WHEN ADAM WAS A BOY

By the same author

THE DISTANT SCENE

UNDER THE PARISH LANTERN

HAWTHORN HEDGE COUNTRY

THE SECRETS OF BREDON HILL

A LAD OF EVESHAM VALE

GOLDEN SHEAVES, BLACK HORSES

MUDDY BOOTS AND SUNDAY SUITS

WHEN VILLAGE BELLS WERE SILENT

POACHER'S PIE

BY HOOK AND BY CROOK

WHEN ADAM WAS A BOY

by

FRED ARCHER

HODDER AND STOUGHTON
LONDON SYDNEY AUCKLAND TORONTO

The author and publisher wish to thank the Editor of the *Evesham Journal* for permission to use the extract on Coronation celebrations on Bredon Hill on p.112 and the following to reproduce photographs: Frank Court, Mrs Mathews, Lawrence Lagridge, Dorothy Bass, Dorothy Boundy.

British Library Cataloguing in Publication Data

Archer, Fred, *b.1915*
　When Adam was a boy.
　1. Ashton-Underhill, Eng. — Social life and
customs
　I. Title
　942.4'49　　DA690.A815
　ISBN 0 340 24825 4

CONTENTS

For my late father
Tom Archer

1

Plough Monday

Plough Monday next after that Twelfth Tide is past
Bids out with the plough the worst husband is last
If ploughman get hatchet or whip to the skrene
Maids loseth their cock if no water be seen.

FRED BUSHELL FARMED THE TWO HUNDRED AND FIFTY ACRE Manor Farm as his father and grandfather had done before him.

Christmas time in 1910 brought back memories of the winters of his youth when old William Bushell, Fred's grandfather, celebrated the twelve days of Christmas in the old style. No work was done, apart from feeding the cattle, the sheep, the horses and the poultry, until Plough Monday, being the Monday following the twelfth day. In fact William Bushell celebrated the twelfth day as Old Christmas Day, a time of great feasting and drinking when the gentry feasted the farmers and the farmers feasted their labourers.

The Bushell family had been shrewd business men who knew that very little was lost in those twelve short days of sleet, snow and frost. The plough lay idle on the headland, the horses spent the short hours of daylight in the Home Orchard but were fed and watered in the warm stables at the Manor. The corn and chaff in the manger and the clover in the rack was dealt out carefully by John Hunt the carter.

He moved amongst the horses by the light of a horn lantern, feeding them both morning and evening. ' 'Tis a curious custom this January holiday, Master, and I've heard how that Squire William, your grandfather, observed it to the letter.'

'True, John, he was keen on the old customs, the old ways, and in fact the men did have a cockerel for a reward if they rose early to plough on Plough Monday.' Fred Bushell then told his carter that in the old household of William Bushell if the ploughman could get his whip, or ploughstaff, or hatchet, or anything he required in the field, and put it in the fireside before the maid had the kettle on, he would have the Shoretide cock which he and the other men would eat on Shore Tuesday before the fasting of Lent.

'One way to get the men back to work,' John replied.

'Your boy left school at Christmas, John. Where's he going to work?'

'Glad you broached the subject, Master, 'cos the bwoy is so fond of 'osses and he wants me to speak for him at the Croome Hunt stables.'

'Passed standard five I hear and sings in the choir. The parson speaks well of him. Don't let him go there, John.'

'Oh, why, sir?' his carter replied. 'There be scope for getting on under the stud groom as a young strapper, no doubt.'

'That man is not fit to school either horses or the boys under him, he's so cruel. I know because I've had words with the M.F.H. about him. Horse-whipping boys, keeping them cleaning and polishing harness until the small hours. I'll give your boy Adam a job working under you and Jones, the under carter.'

'Thank you, sir, but how much a wick 'cos the groom at the Hunt has offered five bob?'

'Five shillings. I'll pay a sovereign every month,' Mr. Bushell replied. 'He can't start until Plough Monday. It pleases me John to keep up just some of the odd notions of grandfather.'

Adam Hunt arrived at Fred Bushell's stable at half past six on Plough Monday morning ready to work with Jones the under carter.

'You be gwain to drive plough for me, bwoy, so get busy getting the 'osses ready 'cos I know you have helped your father on Saturday mornings.'

Adam nodded his head and croaked out a 'Yes', as he stood not yet quite awake by the stable door. He was a smallish lad with jet black hair cropped short by his father; his face was oval, his skin sallow.

His mother had rigged him up in corduroy breeches, a pair of black leather leggings and some new hob-nailed boots, well dressed with Carr's dubbin. He wore an old jacket, the six-penny purchase from the church rummage sale and a flat cloth cap from the Bon Marche. Over his striped Oxford shirt, collarless, fastened with a stud, he wore a thick cord waistcoat made from one of his father's jackets. A red and white cloth muffler acted as both collar and tie around his neck. A tidy boy well dressed for the land of 1911.

He carried a small flail basket which held his ten o'clock bait, the top of a cottage loaf, a piece of hard cheese and a couple of onions. A screw-topped beer bottle in the frail was full of tea, still warm from the pot. Adam knew it would be cold by bait time so on that cold morning he took a swig as soon as Jones had gone up the ladder into the tallet to fork more clover down into the hay rack. Jones wore a pair of yellow velvet cords strapped with leather yorks just below the knee. The broad rim of the trilby hat given him by Mr. Bushell was handy to stick his clay pipe under when he wasn't smoking.

'Start and get the gears on bwoy, we have got to be on the way to the Thurness by seven o'clock,' Jones called from the tallet.

Adam spoke to the horses as they fed from the chaff and corn in the manger. In fact by six thirty the horses had almost finished eating their breakfast for Jones had fed them soon after five o'clock. A hurricane lamp swung from a broken plough trace near the metal corn bin. Adam opened the bin, saw it was half full of crushed oats, then let the lid fall with a bang. All four horses in Jones's part of the stable turned their heads and looked at Adam, expecting him to dole out more corn in the peck measure Jones used.

He knew their names as he knew the names of the horses in his father's stable adjoining. Boxer, Captain, Flower and Violet. Captain was eight years old and would be the filler in the plough team. He was hitched next to the plough—an anchor man.

Hearing Jones coming down the ladder from the tallet above, Adam took Captain's collar off a wooden peg sticking out of the white-washed wall in the gear house and carried it towards the manger. Boxer stood crossways in the stall and his huge chestnut body prevented Adam from getting to Captain's head as he approached the filler of the team on his near side.

'Over boy,' Adam called as his little hand fell lightly on the rounded rump of Boxer. The horse just shuffled away letting Adam through to the manger. As Adam raised the collar in the upside down position towards Captain's head, the horse raised his head higher so that the plough boy couldn't reach. 'All right then old fella,' Adam said climbing into the manger and in no time at all Captain's collar was fixed against his shoulders.

'You ought to go and stand in the bull pen on the bull muck, that 'ud make thee grow bwoy,' Jones said with a laugh as the boy climbed down from the manger.

Adam unhung Captain's mullen from its peg, climbed into the manger, persuaded the horse to open his stubborn mouth, and bridled the filler horse. 'Look sharp and put the collars and mullens on the tother three, 'cos thee bisn't mon enough to put the long gears on um,' Jones said firmly to his young ploughboy.

After the horses had been watered at the stone trough below the pump, Adam hooked the team in line, putting the hooks of the traces of the foremost horse, Boxer, into the ring on the harness of the lash horse, or second in the team, the mare, Violet, whose traces were hooked to Flower's harness, while Flower's traces were hooked to Captain's harness.

Captain wore a cart saddle beside his other gears. The cart saddle held the ridge chain of the plough traces. 'Up, bwoy!' Jones called as he gave Adam a leg up onto Boxer's back. Adam's flail basket was hung on Boxer's harness underneath a brand new whip from Mr. Hine, the local saddler.

Jones walked beside the team carrying a plough paddle, or a miniature spade to clean the sticky clay off the share and mould board of the plough. Hooked on the plough, the team stood patiently on the headland waiting for Adam to click his tongue, a signal for the team to start work.

'Go head,' Jones said and Adam led Boxer ploughing the first furrow towards an elm tree on the opposite headland, a mark Jones had pointed out to him to aim at. The plough slid through the sticky clay leaving a wake of yellow turned stubble, unbroken stretch furrow, as the ploughmen called it.

'How many acres in Thurness?' Adam asked Jones.

'Twenty-two, bwoy. We ull be yer till Candlemas, I reckon,' came the reply.

After the first two furrows were turned, ten chains long, to Hammer and Length, that allotment land on the turnpike road towards Evesham, Adam drove the team. Boxer walked in the newly ploughed trench followed by the other three horses in line.

'Speak to Violet, bwoy, her unt doing her shot,' Jones called to Adam.

'Kup me girl, think I stole ya,' Adam spoke to the mare in a manner learnt from his father. He then raised the whip and cracked it sounding like a rifle shot in the cold still air of January.

'That's it, bwoy,' Jones said, 'but don't thee strike the 'osses uth that persuader you, 'cos if Master Bushell sees any semblance of a weal on their arses there ull be Hell to pay.'

Adam's heavy boots loaded with the sticky clay hung heavy on his young legs and bait time came none too soon. The man and boy sat on a corn sack under the burra of the leafless blackthorn hedge. Adam watched the carter deftly cutting his bread and cheese with a bone-handled shut knife. He had seen his Dad eat in the same way; an inbred art it was the way a sliver of cheese was poised on a thumb piece of bread and fed into the carter's mouth.

Adam walked the stubble up and down, ding-dong, until a quarter to three in the afternoon.

'That ull do for today, but you can't do too much for a good master.'

The plough traces were unhooked from Captain's harness and hung on the hake of the plough at the front end of the beam. Adam mounted Boxer and turned the little caravan of horses towards the gate then along the turnpike road up the Groaten Lane to Mr. Bushell's stable. The trace harness jingled as the horses made for home at a good pace. Jones smoked a clay nosewarmer of Red Bell tobacco.

Adam was used to the scent of Red Bell, his Dad smoked it in the evening, but like Mr. Bushell he rarely smoked at work in the day. As Jones looked at Adam on the foremost horse he thought, a tidy bwoy, well breeched up, a credit to Mrs. Hunt. At the stable Adam helped to ungear the horses and hang up the harness. Jones fed them from the corn bin with a peck measure and filled the hay rack. Then they went to dinner.

Adam's potatoes, greens and mutton were sadly dry in the oven when Mrs. Hunt put his plate on the table. But he ate it with relish, for the cold air, the walking, the cracking of the whip and the old familiar talk to the horses had given him an appetite.

There was little need for Jones to tell his ploughboy which way to drive the team for as long as Adam could remember his Dad's call of 'Turn Jinkum' (to the right) and 'Turn come again' (left), 'Cummy back, ga back, hold back' were as much a part of Adam's everyday speech as the Creed was at church on Sunday.

After a week of driving the plough team up and down the furrow of the Thurness Field, Adam's little hands became chapped from the cold January winds. His feet were sore with chilblains and despite the fact that he soaked them every night in ivy water he cried every morning when the strong hob-nailed boots were pulled over his thick woollen stockings.

Mrs. Hunt boiled ivy leaves in an old saucepan, a remedy for chilblains handed down from the time when she was in service. The liquor did ease the pain in Adam's swollen toes and those early nights to bed under the thatch were spent sleeping, dreaming of the day when he could be a ploughman.

'He don't need no rocking to sleep when he climbs the wooden hill at nine o'clock,' his father remarked to Mrs. Hunt. ' 'Tis like breaking in 'osses. When 'osses gets used to the collar, work comes second nature.'

'Don't thee compare my bwoy to a 'oss, John, it unt a kind thing to do.'

Adam's Dad laughed, puffed a cloud of smoke from his clay pipe as he sat under the ingle, then said, 'Collar proud,' and chuckled to himself.

'I know what you mean, John Hunt, and you was a bwoy once and no doubt collar proud then a day.'

'Ah, the green 'osses shoulders be teart on Monday mornings, as my old Dad used to say. What dost reckon kills old 'osses Missus?' John Hunt asked teasing her as the two were drinking their supper cocoa.

'I don't know nor care,' she replied, 'but I'm gwain to see that my bwoy has plenty of fittle and drink and a warm bed. What kills um John?'

'Starting work again,' he replied, 'and that applies to we mortals, 'cos when a mon gives up his usual half past six till half past five labour in the fields for a while, 'tis hard grind to start work again.'

'Talking now like some old gaffer be ya and thee bist only thirty-five year old. Time past thee wast along of Master Bushell on the District Council.'

The evening following Adam came home from the furrows of Thurness tired after tramping the miles which he had covered ploughing one acre in the day.

'Just fetch a bucket of water from the pump, bwoy,' his Dad exclaimed as Adam sank his corduroyed backside into the softness of the sofa.

'Have a care now, John, let the bwoy eat his fittle,' Mrs. Hunt said with feeling.

'All right then, I suppose I shall have to fetch it. That's the maxim then is it, wear the old uns out first?'

Coming back into the kitchen, John clanked the galvanised bucket down on the stone slabbed floor under the brown crock sink. He sat down at his place at the table next to Adam, turned towards him and with a wry smile said, 'Ah, every generation gets weaker and wiser.'

Mrs. Hunt raised her eyebrows, looked quite serious as she replied, 'Our Adam unt weak but the bwoy is but thirteen year old.'

John pursued his point still further saying, 'I'll tell tha what Missus. I ploughed with a pair of 'osses when I was eleven and 'tis time Adam learnt how to hold the plough tails and the rope G.O. reins.'

'I can plough Dad. Jones will tell ya, 'cos often I hold the plough and Jones drives the team and turn on the headland.'

'I'll see Mr. Bushell in the morning, the stubble near Great Hill Barn will have to ploughed next wick.'

'Not by me up there on my own,' Adam replied.

'There's another bwoy starting on Monday. He's only twelve but his widowed mother needs the feow coppers wages. He's gwain to drive plough for Jones and thee and me can plough the Barn Hill with two pair of 'osses.'

Mrs. Hunt looked with pride on her boy and said, 'How about that, Adam, ploughing with two horses on your own.'

Adam didn't speak, but just smiled and looked at his Dad.

'Now John,' Mrs. Hunt said, 'Just be easy on the bwoy and let him have a couple of good horses out of your stable 'cos I know how you keep the best for yourself.'

'He can have Noble and Merriman, there's a pair sensible as Christians.'

'Which ones'll you be working then, Dad?' Adam remarked knowing that the two he mentioned were the pick of the stable.

'Ah, I'm in for a bending for a feow days breaking in young Blackbird and Prince, the two black three-year-olds. They've worked in a tandem team and I've had them pulling the duckfeet drag harrows, now they must plough abreast.'

Mrs. Hunt who knew almost as much about horses as John, having worked in service on a big farm and with other girls helped with the haymaking, looked at her husband saying as if amused, 'A smartish caper you ull cut with two half broken three-year-olds.'

John was peeved at this remark feeling that the rise was being taken out of him. He puffed at his pipe then took it from his mouth, pointed the stem to his wife then to Adam, and said, 'Dost think I'm fool enough to take two young 'osses together until they have got used to the plough.' Hesitating he said, 'Perhaps you do, but I'm working Blackbird with the old mare Pleasant for a feow days then working Prince with the old mare for a while until he's useful. Afterwards the two can work together as a pair.'

In 1911 it was the ambition of some of the boys leaving their village school to drive the great steam railway engines which just ate up the miles on the iron roads of England. Starting life as cleaners and greasers in the engine sheds then becoming firemen on some non-descript goods engine, but always reaching up towards the top hoping, longing, to drive a fast locomotive on the main arterial lines to London. The shining green monsters on the Great Western were admired by Adam and his friends as they steamed through Evesham station shaking the little footbridge which led to platform two.

Adam was not to be wooed by the railways at a time when they were at their peak. He knew that his place would be on the land where his father worked. Maybe one day he could drive the great steam cultivating engines ploughing six furrows at a time or even the small portable engine that drove the threshing machine. One wonders what thoughts, what emotions sprang up in the mind of a boy of thirteen about to handle two horses and a plough.

Fred Bushell was in the stable yard early on the Monday morning when the Hunts were to plough Barn Hill. He watched his head carter gear up old Pleasant and young Blackbird, in fact, he helped John to harness Blackbird who pottered about outside the stable like a circus horse.

Adam stood beside Noble and Merriman both staid and trusted geldings. He wasn't too concerned about his Dad as he waltzed around with Blackbird until he fixed the coupling stick between the ring on his bit and the one on Pleasant's bridle.

'Green he is, Master, but I ull make him foam at his shoulders, mane and tail by knocking off time.'

'Don't overdo him, John, the first day.' Then smiling, Fred Bushell turned to Adam and said, 'Your Dad's got two to break in today but I think you will manage that little Ransome plough, won't you?'

'Yes sir, I held the Kell plough in the Thurness with Jones,' the boy replied.

Fred Bushell had broken in more horses and boys than he had had Christmas dinners. Bailiff he had been on a big estate, a man with compassion for horses and men. 'Now John,' Mr. Bushell said, 'I want the Barn Hill ploughed. Don't fetch the stones on the top but bury the stubble as well as you can.'

'Always have done a decent job, haven't I, Master?'

Fred Bushell nodded as man and boy walked up through the young orchard, then up through Paris hamlet on to Bredon Hill.

'Dust want to ride, Adam?' John spoke to his son by Boss Close gate, ' 'cos thee ut be walking all day.'

Adam smiled as his father gave him a leg up on to Noble's back. 'I a got a walk no alonside this unequal pair. Tortoise and hare race today, happen.'

On Great Hill the pair left the cart track taking a footpath to Great Hill Barn. Here Adam tied his horses to the yard fence and held Blackbird and Pleasant while his Dad wheeled out of the cart shed a handy little Ransome plough.

'There, bwoy, that's thy new toy for today and now I'll fetch my tool out, my Kell plough.'

'Why do you use a Kell, Dad?' Adam asked.

'One thing me and Master Bushell agrees on. Kells of Gloucester make the best ploughs for around Bredon.'

After this John Hunt untied Adam's pair from the railings and hooked them to the Ramsome plough. 'Just hold on to my two craters for a while and I'll strike out a few beds of ploughing with Noble and Merriman.'

Adam sat under the wall of the barn ground with a rope rein in his hand attached to Blackbird, while he watched his Dad plough the first furrows.

'There now, you can help me to start with my two. Noble and Merriman will stand as quiet as two old sheep in the furrow, just lead old Pleasant across the field and I'll see what sort of a fist can be made with Blackbird as her partner.'

Adam led the old mare, John tried to keep Blackbird in check with the G.O. reins, but he tugged and snatched in the traces always a couple of yards in front of Pleasant. 'I'll manage now, bwoy,' John told his son. 'I've set your plough, thur's no need to tug the reins while Noble's in the furrow. Turn gently on the headland and talk to um in a quiet voice. No shouting mind.'

Adam found ploughing his first furrow the satisfaction which is the lot of every ploughman. The creak of the harness, the jingle of the brasses, the smell of the newly turned earth. He imitated his father's measured step, the near yard stride.

The January days on Bredon Hill grew longer after the middle of the month. As the two teams climbed the hill in the morning, Adam noticed that at first the early light of dawn appeared as they passed the spring of water in the walled tussocky field before they reached the barn ground. Ten days later the morning star still shone over the Cotswold edge as the horses plodded up the well worn track through the gully at Paris.

The oil lamplit window of Tom the poacher's camp house gave a yellow light across the rough road. 'Cromwell tied his hoss up there Dad, didn't he?'

The words of young Adam brought a laugh from John Hunt as he said, 'Oi bwoy, and thur's another such rogue as bides there now; Tom the poacher.'

Fred Bushell paid his men every month. He met them in the yard on the Saturday afternoon when they knocked off at four o'clock. Men on the farm in 1911 worked six days a week but were allowed home early on Saturday afternoon.

John Hunt was responsible for looking after and feeding the horses on Sundays. The custom had been for stockmen to be given a breakfast on Sunday mornings for looking after the animals. Fred Bushell continued the practice of his father, providing a meal of home cured bacon, with fresh baked bread and cider from the hogshead barrels in the barn.

Adam never forgot his first pay day when the Master handed to him one golden sovereign for the four weeks' work, slipping it into his breeches pocket with his left hand and grasping the coin tightly, never taking his hand from his pocket until he reached the cottage and then handing it to his mother. How proud he felt beggars description when Mrs. Hunt threw her arms around her son and gave him a shilling pocket money.

Maybe a simple phase in the life of a country boy, but no doubt his mother was proud too knowing that Adam at thirteen was working two horses with a plough nine hundred feet up Bredon Hill along-side his father in January, when, as John Hunt used to say, 'The skinny wind from Rushia goes through ya. No hills yer between us and the Ural mountains.'

One morning when the hoar frost showed its rime on the stunted hawthorn trees, Adam noticed that it was lighter at half past seven as the ploughmen passed the Paris Barn. He said so to his father who with his father before him had seen some severe winters on the hill. 'Ah, bwoy, as the days lengthen the cold strengthens.' John thought awhile then added, 'T'won't be much warmer till Valentine's, that's when winter's back breaks as a rule.'

At three o'clock as Adam and his father made their way to the Manor stables through the gardens of Paris they saw Jones with his four horse team walking up the Groaten from the Thurness field. They met in the stable yard, two men, two boys and eight horses. Pulling his great turnip watch from his waistcoat pocket, Adam's Dad said to Jones, the under carter, 'Judged that well didn't ya, bwoy, 'tis on the stroke of three.'

Jones walked his four heavy shires through the shallow pond by the gate and he and the boy were busy washing the clay off the feathers of their hooves. Then, he and the boy each took a rick peg and scraped their heavy boots. 'Loving yunt it, you,' John Hunt said to Jones in his usual waggish way.

'Oi, 'tis clinging, the Thurness clay; you chaps on the hill be lucky. A gentleman's life ploughing that brash ground,' Jones replied.

'Have ya amus finished the Thurness?' the head carter asked his under carter, knowing full well that from the hill he could see some acres of unploughed stubble. Jones made no reply until John made a comment he had often heard made by his father when a job seemed to take a long time, 'Costing our gaffer summat working the Thurness this year, don't the job begin to stink.'

'Talks as your belly guides ya, like an old apple woman you do, John. I be in no mood for such nonsense.'

Adam and the other boy got on with their work ungearing the horses. John climbed the tallet ladder and tossed more leafy clover with his fork into the hay rack.

January was almost over for 1911 when Jones ploughed the headland in Thurness and Adam and his Dad finished ploughing Barn Hill. Adam was sad to leave the hill for he enjoyed the solitude, the feeling of being above the Vale village, above the fogs of winter in the clear crisp air of a walled in landscape.

He sat on a corn sack under the beech trees in the shelter of a stone wall to eat his ten o'clock bait. Here he built a fire of fallen beech and larch wood and once or twice a week his mother gave him a rasher of home-cured bacon to cook over the fire on a nut stick toasting fork. Catching the fat as it dripped from the rasher on his bread, it was here that Adam tasted a richer life than that he was used to at school.

By late January the larks sang from the half light of morning throughout the day while the peewits followed close to the plough searching for wire worms. In the clump of beech trees the rooks were already building or rather, restoring their rough twig nests ready to hold the March eggs and the April young.

Plough Monday seemed a long while ago to Adam, so much had happened. Now a ploughboy had become a ploughman in just a month. This one sovereign a month boy was promised a four shilling rise by Mr. Bushell. Cheap labour it could be said, but Adam was being apprenticed to the oldest and most worthwhile calling on the land.

His two-horse team, Noble and Merriman, had been broken in by his father, and now guided Adam along the straight furrows marked out by his ancestors. He had worked on a hill from where he could see the smoke of engines on two railways and could hear the roar of the expresses on the main line from Birmingham to Bristol as they sped through the little stations of Eckington and Bredon. The little tank engines which pushed and pulled the Midland trains along the branch line to and from Evesham puffed out of Ayshon station with clocklike regularity. The twenty to ten passenger to Evesham every morning was a signal that in another two or three bouts of ploughing bait time at ten o'clock was due. The twenty past two told Adam that the late dinner knocking off time was near.

Over the Vale as Adam looked towards the Cotswolds he saw the smoke from the engines on what the locals called the new line from Honeybourne junction to Cheltenham. The smoke laid a trail along the edge of the hills as the trains steamed past Laverton Halt. Adam had seen it all before when he had followed the Croome hounds in the Christmas holidays from Elmley Park, past the Tower known as Parson's Folly, down to Eckington withy beds by the Avon river. He watched the smoke of the new line until it disappeared when the trains entered the tunnel under the hills. Was it his uncle driving the Bristol to Birmingham express? As a little boy his mother had taken him to New Street station and he had stood on the footplate of his uncle's engine.

'Cup Merriman!' Adam called turning the horses on the headland. No time for imagination he thought, can't do too much for a good master. The share of the plough bit into the earth scraping the limestone underneath. The railway's just a timekeeper for me he thought.

2

Candlemas

CANDLEMAS DAY, FEBRUARY 2ND, WAS AN AGRICULTURAL landmark on the Manor Farm of Fred Bushell. He knew that winter was far from over. He recited the old sayings of his father, 'The farmer should have on Candlemas Day half his straw and half his hay.' It was evident that fine weather at this season was looked upon with a fear of bad weather to come. Fine weather in February is known as a 'weather breeder.'

> Foul weather is no news, hail, rain and snow .
> Are now expected and esteemed no woe.
> Nay 'tis an omen bad the yeomen say
> If Phoebus shows his face the second day.
> On Candlemas Day if the sun shines clear
> The shepherd had rather see his wife on the bier
> If Candlemas Day be fine and clear
> Corn and fruits will then be dear.

The great horse fair at Evesham at Candlemas was one of the most important events in the farming year for Fred Bushell. His horses were looked upon as the finest examples of shires in Gloucestershire. He bred foals from brood mares sired by Harold, a stallion known in the book as top in his class.

The Birmingham merchants, iron masters like Jim Cambridge, brewers and the Midland Railway, looked for five-year-olds from Fred's stable, knowing to buy from him was to own the very best in horse flesh. The ways of Fred Bushell were patterned by this sale of five-year-olds and in two years' time Prince and Blackbird would be sold at Candlemas Fair as five-year-old geldings, 'sound in wind and limb, no vices, fit for town work, work in all gears'. That's of course if Adam's Dad was able to get them useful in chains and shafts.

Fred Bushell was indeed a farmer a cut above his neighbours in the Vale. He lived amongst the apple orchards which were a sea of blossom in the springtime under Bredon Hill. He farmed the Manor Farm, but was more of a yeoman than Lord of the Manor.

The very appearance of Mr. Bushell suggested that he may have descended from the Great Protector, or Fellow Peasant, Oliver Cromwell. His talk was not intellectual as reckoned in university, but to sit there in his kitchen with hams and flitches on the racks above, and mugs of cider on the scrubbed table, was illuminating. Fred Bushell's education was little more than that of the carter, John Hunt, but his stock of intuition was amazing. Not only was Fred a son of the soil, it seemed that he was a part of it. His logic was that without the farmer being at one with his land, the land was poor and the farmer poor. So Mr. Bushell, lord or peasant, had tilled the land farmed by his father before him since he had left an estate on the other side of the hill where he had been bailiff.

Old Mr. Bushell insisted that Fred should have his feet under someone else's table for a few years and farm independent of him. Bailiffs have always been accused of mixing the sugar with the sand; that is, marketing livestock and corn belonging to the landlord and keeping some of the proceeds, also accepting backhanders from dealers—outrights or outriders, in the trade. Fred was shrewd, a good haggler at market, a hard bargainer, but honest. 'Right's right and might's might, but wrong's no man's right,' was his maxim.

When he came to farm the Manor on the death of his father, the farm was suddenly transformed. The hedges were trimmed, the land drained and on land where his father had muddled along, a pattern and order was restored. The conversation in the White Hart where Singer Sallis was landlord had been critical of where Fred Bushell had made his money. 'The old man never left much 'cos his will was in the *Journal*. Just over a thousand,' one customer said.

'Ah,' Bert Chandler said, 'but our gaffer married one of Nehemiah's daughters from Elmley and he had got a bob or two.' Bert Chandler was shepherd for Mr. Bushell and he and young Ruby, Fred's son, looked after the cattle as well as the sheep on the hill.

By 1911 the Manor Farm was carrying a sizeable flock of Cotswold sheep on Bredon Hill and store and fat cattle down in Brook Meadow. Bert Chandler was a lean corduroyed figure with collarless Oxford shirt and a scrawny weather beaten neck partly covered by a red muffler. His manner of speech was peculiar. Hoarse and hesitating at first, as though the physical effort was difficult, then rising now and then when he stressed a point into the characteristic crescendo. Presently his voice would sink to a deep and resonant note as he uttered, well known to his friends, one of his Chandler phrases — 'You understand my meaning,' 'There you are, you know what I mean,' 'That's a funny thing.'

These ways Bert had in speaking in riddles took some getting used to, but Fred Bushell and his son Ruby knew that their stockman shepherd was trying to explain a difficult situation. His tone of subdued emphasis was certainly impressive, a mastery of a manner of utterance, convincing by its quiet indifference to effect. A rustic mystic whose appearance gave little indication of the depth of his thoughts or his capabilities.

With the Bushell flock of Cotswold sheep penned with withy hurdles in the yard of the Cross Barn, Bert looked over his flock much as a medical specialist would look at patients under his care. He would stand there, leaning against a hurdle, his short clay pipe sticking out of his mouth at right angles to his profile, as if watching the glowing twist tobacco in the bowl, while all the time he was contemplating whether a certain ewe which had lost her lamb was worth considering mating with the tup in September or should she go to an Evesham butcher.

'Didn't give enough milk did you, old girl,' he muttered to himself, then he pasted a red mark made with raddle on the ewe's rump. 'Won't risk you this time, I got to cull a feow.' With his crook Bert Chandler then hooked the left leg of the ewe. She came towards him on the other three legs and was put in the other pen along with the barren ewes for the butcher.

During the late February lambing in the Cross Barn Bert never slept in a bed for a month. He left the barn for an hour or so in the middle of the night and what he called slummocked down on the sofa in his cottage covered with a horse blanket. In the barn he sat and read by the stove between the frequent confinements of the ewes. *Tit Bits* and *John Bull*.

Being the man he was, a stickler for things being right, the comments in *John Bull* about the indiscretions of our rulers in Government were meat and drink to him, but Bert was a faithful follower of Lloyd George and disagreed with any criticism of him by *John Bull's* open letters 'without fear or favour'.

Bert liked nothing better than to discuss things in general with his master. Fred Bushell did relieve his shepherd some evenings in the lambing pen, sending him home at six o'clock until ten, but Bert often stopped a while, telling his employer which ewes to watch or warning him that a certain ewe with some wool off her neck had been 'on the job', as he called lambing, for too long for his liking, and to 'look out for a lamb with a leg back in the lamb bed', as he called the womb.

One February morning Mr. Bushell had sent Jones and young Adam to the barn to thatch some hurdles with straw and make what was known as burra hurdles to shelter the lambs in the yard from the late snowfall. Jones and Adam worked with a ball of binder twine, placing the long wheat straw as they opened the boltins against the withy hurdles, then tying them to spars.

Bert Chandler detested any other workmen on the farm entering his barn at lambing time. 'Strangers do upset my yows,' he said. As the snow fell deep in the orchard outside Bert reasoned that it would have been better for the hurdles to be thatched in the dutch barn, then brought to him on a dray. As Fred Bushell arrived he sensed that Bert was unusually quiet. 'Quiet this morning, Bert,' Fred said as he opened the big double door of the barn.

'I be quiet, Master, I'll allow,' but, looking towards Jones and Adam he said, 'if you use this un too much,' touching his lips with his forefinger, 'you soon gets accused of using this un,' touching his nose.

'I see,' Fred replied with a laugh, knowing full well that his shepherd didn't wish to divulge anything to Jones and Adam and neither did he want to know their business.

A young ewe in the corner of the pen was bleating lying down, straining, then running around and lying down again. 'Have a look at this yow, Master. Her's barely two year old and it does look like her can't lamb.' Bert caught the young ewe and lay her on the straw. 'Hers broke her waters a while ago but nothing shows yet. My hand's too big to put in her passage. 'Tis a pity the missus unt yer. Her's very handy with her small hand at drawing a big lamb from a young yow.'

'How about Adam?' Mr. Bushell said looking towards the farthest bay in the big barn where he was thatching hurdles.

'I unt partial to having gallus young devils like him among the yows. They be dilicate compared with the 'osses.'

'Come, come, Bert, let the boy have a try.'

'All right, as long as he does what I say.'

Adam, as he went towards the ewe pen wondered why he was sent for, knowing that Bert Chandler had no time for boys in his barn. 'Try and get this lamb, bwoy, but first wash your hands in disinfectant in that bucket.'

Adam did as he was told. Mr. Bushell held the ewe's head while Bert Chandler held her hind legs. 'Hold her, Master, while I get the soap and the water off the stove. Well lather your hands bwoy and I'll put some green oils in her passage. Now I want you to hold on to both feet of the lamb and pull down.'

Adam, doing as he was told, slid his little hand inside the ewe, then said, 'I've got both legs, Mr. Chandler.'

'Pull steady every time the yow strains.'

Adam soon had two little feet outside the ewe's passage. Bert slipped his finger and found that the lamb's head was coming, but let Adam finish lambing the ewe. It was a ram lamb, so could be a stock-getter next year.

'There Bert, you know Adam has saved one life, perhaps two,' Mr. Bushell said.

'Good bwoy you be, Adam, and they tells me you be still in the church choir.'

'Yes, Mr. Chandler, I do sometimes take the solo parts,' Adam replied.

'Seen it in the *Journal* I have and had to smile when I read, "The solo was sung by Master Adam Hunt." Takes me back a bit, Adam, to the time when I was a boy soprano.'

'Parson came to see you when you were laid up with bronchitis before Christmas, didn't he?' Fred Bushell made this remark to tease his old shepherd knowing that the parson and the shepherd were what Bert called, 'Not first cousins.' Never seeing eye to eye. 'I'd bin devilish middling for three wicks ya know, Gaffer. You brought me a bottle of whisky and had jellies and blancmanges and biff tay sent round. I was on the mend, amus fit for work when the parson came along. You know, Master, I never had much education, unt much of a scholard so to speak, never as much as rubbed my back against a college wall, but I can hold my own with the parson, Master of Arts, Bachelor of Arts.'

Fred Bushell laughed, knowing that his shepherd was once more talking in riddles about college walls and so on.

'B.A. he put after his name and M.A. Now I heard a chap preach at the chapel, an ordinary working chap off the farm, and he said he had got a B.A. and an M.A. Then he explained. He reckoned he had bin Born Again and Marvellously Altered. Now unt that a licker, Master?'

'Come on, Bert, we must be off. I must, in fact, and Adam must get back to hurdle thatching, but what happened when the parson visited you? Went away with his tail between his legs I reckon.'

'Ya see, he started telling me that he had got a flock of four hundred to shepherd, then he asked me how many we had at the Manor. I said 'twas about two hundred and forty yows, all Cotswolds. He looked at me devilish cocky so to speak. I was sat in the chair beside the bed when he brought the usual tin of cocoa and he got the Missus to open it so that he could have the coupon.'

'What did you tell him, Bert?' Mr. Bushell pressed the question.

'I be getting round to it, but you understand my meaning when I say to Adam, this is on the Q.T. mind, don't thee tell a soul.'

Adam nodded. Bert at last told his master and the boy that he replied to the parson by telling him straight he didn't think much of the way he did his shepherding. 'If I didn't get around my sheep any more often than you gets around yours, udn't my yows have some maggots in their fleeces. I bin abed for three wicks, sir, afore you come to shepherd me. My flock get shepherded twice a day.'

As Fred Bushell left the barn, Bert was guiding the newly lambed ewe into a little hurdled pen six foot by three where she licked her lamb dry. Soon the lamb's curly coat changed from the yellow slime of birth to white, as white as its mother's, and it was on its feet sucking the warm curds from its mother's udder.

'I'll be along tonight at six, Bert, to give you a break,' Mr. Bushell called from the door.

'Oi, all right, Gaffer. Daresay the missus ull be glad to see me for an hour or so,' his shepherd replied.

Fanny Chandler was a busy little woman. She and Bert lived in a cottage smelling of Lifebuoy soap and moth balls, scrubbed so clean Bert often boasted, 'You could eat your fittle off the floor in our place.' Ready for Bert's arrival home at six o'clock when her man was more than thirsty for a cup of tea, she had the tea pot stewing on the hob of the oven grate. As Bert scuffed his hob-nailed boots on the stone-flagged floor in the passage, she poured him out his first cup of tea. She then saucered it and blew it until it was cool enough to drink. 'Queen Victoria saucered her tea,' she always said as an excuse.

Fanny Chandler made butter in the Bushells' dairy and was allowed a little every week. She spread some on some crusty home-made bread, then plastered a little blackberry jam on what she called his piece. This was Bert's tea.

1911 was a special year for Bert Chandler, the last year he shepherded the Bushell Cotswold ewes. At the cottage that lambing time Tom discussed with his wife plans when they would live on the pension he called the Lloyd George and a little allowance Mr. Bushell had promised him on top of a rent free cottage.

'Young Ruby's a gwain to look after the ship. He's folding the tegs on the turnip up on Bredon now a day. Rides up the hill on that shaggy cob, the one with the white star in front of his face.'

'Can he lamb a yow Bert?' Fanny said knowing how that her husband was a past master in the lambing pen.

'He's coming along to the barn next wick and I'm gwain to give him the rudiments. Ah Ruby ull be all right if he don't get entangled with the women.'

Fanny Chandler from the kitchen sink said to her husband, 'What do you think of that Mildred of his then, Bert? Do you reckon she ull steady Ruby down? 'Cos 'tween women and drink he's a gallus young torrel, ya know.'

'Maybe,' Bert replied. 'Now, speaking as a man, and an old man,

Mildred ud turn the yud of any fellow. I'll allow some of her beauty does stem from the paint pot, but I'll go to Hanover if her unt a useful filly. That wave in her hair, her bowsams do stand out and her be corsetted at the waist like a wasp. I'd like about forty miles with her on a truckload of straw behind the banana train.'

'I never asked for that, Bert, but I suppose you be the same as the rest, looking at the women like Fred Bushell looks at his fat cattle. She's a very passionate girl, I'll agree, but there is a gentle side to her nature. She can make a fellow feel he's the only one for her. Like that engine driver from Cleeve.'

'What about him then, Missus?'

. 'Ah, she was at the funeral after he was killed on the line at Ashchurch. He was the son of a Beckford guard, so they buried him at Beckford. When the coffin was lowered into the ground and as the mourners walked away, Mildred Churchway dropped a lovely red rose on the coffin and said for all to hear, "He was the only man that was ever any good to me." '

'How's Ruby going to follow that then?' Bert replied.

Fred Bushell's field by Great Hill Barn had been described by Bert Chandler 'as poor as Job's heart'. The constant growing of oats by Fred's father had impoverished the ground, so that the corn field was insufficient for keeping the horses.

Tom Bowman and Harry Carter were partners market gardening and farming a rented farm adjoining the Manor. Their special strain of sprouts was noted for miles around. Up until 1911 no one had ever dared grow sprouts up on the Bredon or Cotswold Hills. Tom and Harry sat in Fred Bushell's kitchen one February night after a day's rabbiting on Fred's Bredon Hill land. 'What are you planting by Great Hill Barn, Mr. Bushell?' Harry questioned with interest. 'The ground looks kind and lies nicely in the furrow.'

'Ah Harry, that fifteen acres is going in with turnips.' Then turning to Ruby, his son, he added, 'I want a truckload of bag muck took up on Bredon and sowed next week.'

'Right, Dad, but who's to sow it? I'm busy helping Bert with the lambing.'

'There's Tustin Finch. He can leave the hedge laying in Thurness and work on the Hill.'

Ruby nodded and wondered how long it would take Tustin to sow the fertiliser.

'I'd just like to plant sprouts by Great Hill Barn, wouldn't you Harry?' Tom Bowman said to his partner. Harry Carter, the older of the two men by ten years, stroked his greying moustache then popped a somewhat impulsive question to Mr. Bushell, 'Will you let Tom and me rent that fifteen acres and we will plant it?'

Fred Bushell smiled as he looked at the two market gardeners. 'There's rabbits up on the hill by the hundred Harry,' he ventured.

'I'll see to them,' Harry Carter replied. 'What sort of bag muck is in the truck at Ashton station?' he continued.

'Superphosphate of lime,' Ruby said, 'seven and a half tons.'

Tom Bowman looked at Harry who gave him a wink, then turned to Fred with these words. 'Tom and I will buy the artificial off you and pay you a good rent.'

'What do you think, Ruby?' his father asked him.

'Well, Father, we need the greens for the tegs in the spring, but if it's sprouts on the hill I can hitch the yearling lambs on the stems as we do with the turnips.'

So it came about that Bowman and Carter ventured to grow sprouts nearly one thousand feet up on Bredon. Ruby and Tustin Finch loaded the carts with superphosphate at the little station and helped by Jones, the under carter, the three men with six horses climbed the rough rocky road to Great Hill Barn. Here Tustin Finch sowed the fertiliser known as artificial, or bag muck, while with two horses and a set of zig-zag harrows young Adam worked it into the ground.

'The stone is pretty near the top soil, Tom,' Harry Carter said as they walked across the field with their guns at the edge of night. Tom agreed and replied, 'I've an idea to get more mould for the plants to root in but we'll discuss that in the morning.'

Harry looked across the Vale below. The cathedral tower of Gloucester was still in sight, but the dusk fell like a closing curtain on the hill. The rabbits were leaving their burrows, or holts as Harry called them, like a little army of furry men approaching the greening sainfoin field adjoining the Barn Field.

'Are you worried about the rabbits eating our plants, Tom?' Harry asked in his usual breezy way.

'You say you can deal with them, Harry, so I'm not bothered,' Tom answered.

Harry took two crimson flash cartridges from his jacket pocket and slid them into the breech of his double-barrel gun. 'Are you loaded,' he called to Tom, who just nodded looking at the rabbits grazing the sainfoin. 'Follow me,' Harry said and crouching down low he made for the stone wall. Here the two men cocked the hammers of their guns. Harry whispered, 'Now, Tom, shoot when I say. Right,' he said under his breath.

Four shots were fired at the rabbits. In the fading light the partners climbed the wall, picked up six of the finest rabbits. Reared and fed on the sparse pasture of Bredon they still measured up to what Squire Parsons had said years ago when Bredon Hill rabbits were called as one of the cries of London.

'That's six less,' Harry laughingly said as he paunched them and hocked them, hung them on an elder stick, then shouldered the stick. 'Just carry my gun, Tom, 'tis too dark now to shoot again, but I been thinking. Alan Harding who sells the fish under the Town Hall at Evesham will give up eight pence a piece for as many as we can catch. Fred Bushell did ask me to catch them.'

'Why not bring old Durgin Green with you, Harry, to help you set the rabbit wires? He's a wily chap setting a snare.'

'Bit slow, Tom, now, though his wires do put the rabbits' neck-laces on all right. But I'll have to buy some more wires at Averill's in Evesham when I go to market in the morning, then I'll drive over with Min in the dray.'

As Harry and Tom wished each other good night by the Tythe Barn, Harry said, 'What's this idea of yours to get more mould for the plants on the stony ground, eh?'

'Bout the land up with a bouting out plough and plant the sprouts on the ridges.'

'Sounds all right to me; like tater planting you mean?'

'That's it, Harry. I'll speak to Fred Bushell. Our light horses wouldn't manage it.'

A couple of days passed before Harry Carter and old Durgin pegged down two hundred rabbit wires in a kind of arc semicircling the sainfoin thirty yards from the wall and nearly two hundred yards from the rabbit holts. Over the wall in the barn ground young Adam drove two horses pulling a ridging plough, pushing the stony soil into straight ridges ready for the sprout plants.

'There's a boy for you, Durgin. Thirteen year old, ploughing like a veteran, a sight for sore eyes,' Harry said with a chuckle.

On a cold February night Harry and Durgin walked up Bredon by the light of Harry's carbide bicycle lamp to pick up the snared rabbits. Sixty rabbits waited to be bagged by the catchers and there were forty more next morning. Ferreting by day and snaring by night, Harry and old Durgin soon lessened the rabbits on the hill.

1911 was still the age of yeoman farmers working the land around Bredon, a time when the tenants of large estates were vetted by the landlord for being credit-worthy and proved tillers of the soil. Fred Bushell's decision to let land to the two young men of the Vale was somewhat out of the ordinary, but that was Fred Bushell, a man who trusted so few of his fellows but took a liking to the industrious ways of Harry and Tom. Harry Carter and Tom Bowman were alike in one respect only. They were handsome, healthy men of the land.

Harry had bright blue, searching eyes; eyes which saw through the thoughts of the merchants and growers he dealt with. His brown hair was greying at the temples, his moustache was tightly clipped. On market days he dressed in grey tweed breeches, cloth gaiters, light black boots he called his tea-drinkers, a tweed jacket, fancy waistcoat, starched shirt front and a grey trilby hat.

Few men of Evesham Vale at forty-five years old had gleaned so much of the ways and lore of market gardening the land. Brought up on a farm where he had reaped the corn, milked the cows, he soon rented land at Donnybrook on the outskirts of Evesham town.

He married, built three houses and bought himself a polished wooden governess cart, a steel grey cob and black harness shining with brass. His cob, Dick, was high stepping, impressive. Fred Bushell who was such a lover of good horseflesh was undoubtedly taken by Harry's turnout.

His workaday gear was somewhat different from the showy cob and cart he used for travelling to Tewkesbury or Cheltenham. Min, his nag, drew Harry on his dray with loads of fruit to the railway station. He rarely wore a jacket winter and summer, but could be seen stripped to the shirt on his land or on the dray, growing and hauling his produce to rail for the city. He wouldn't suffer fools gladly. It's fair to say he was impulsive and could get up in the boughs when roused by incompetence or dishonesty in his men, or in fact anyone, but he had the great ability to forgive and forget very soon.

Tom Bowman, ten years younger than Harry was still a bachelor at thirty-five, though he had a young lady called Lily in Donnybrook and was saving prudently for the wedding. He had lost his widowed mother the year before and now lived at Stanley Farm under Bredon Hill. He had recently rented the place off Fred Bushell. Tom was medium height with broad shoulders, rosy cheeks, black hair and a quite heavy, but trimmed black moustache. He wore a brown mixture tweed suit on market days, brown chrome boots, lightly nailed. His soft white collar and spotted tie gave a finish to his Oxford shirt. A check cap gave the impression that he was about to go to a point to point, but neither he nor Harry had time for such luxuries.

Tom drove a nag, also named Tom, and his dray to the fruit market or station and he had bought a similar turnout to his partner. His governess cart was pulled by Polly, a chestnut mare harnessed in brown leather with a little brass. Polly was like her master, quiet, steady and afraid of no one, a trait Tom maintained throughout his life. Tom was a worrier, a solver of sums, a planner of crops, a judge of stock, but left the complexities of growing strawberries, onions and peas to Harry Carter.

There is one more thing these two diverse characters had in common. Working the land, planting, harvesting, making the hay, weighing the peas, they always took their guns, always were accompanied by their dogs — Tom's a liver and white spaniel named Tiny, Harry's an Italian greyhound named Jim. Dogs and guns lay on the headland of the field whilst their masters worked. It's hard to say which man was the better shot, Harry or Tom. Harry could pick a rabbit off with his twelve bore three feet in front of Jim with no danger to his dog. Tom would down the passing pigeon as it sailed high above the hedgerow elms.

As these two men worked together they learnt from each other in a way that no college could teach. Harry had seen the way the Donnybrook gardners cut and packed their cabbage into the withy pot hampers, guessing each package to around sixty pounds weight;

how the women bunched the asparagus buds to be tied in bundles of a hundred by the gardener. He was a past master at that and the dozening of onions by a withy twig; Tom had learnt from Fred Bushell, his neighbour, how to assess and buy the right cattle for fattening.

He had watched and helped Bert Chandler as a boy shepherd Fred Bushell's sheep. He learnt to shear, to drench ewes and calves with medicine. He had ploughed the land under Bredon with John Hunt, Adam's father. Fred Bushell knew Tom as a worker, an industrious up and coming business man and was intrigued by Harry Carter's know how of the growing and marketing of peas, sprouts, beans, plums and strawberries. When Harry took a couple of chips of his selected Joseph Paxton strawberries to the Manor for Fred in his polished governess cart on a July Sunday afternoon in exchange for a pint of fresh cream, there was un understanding between the worker of the Donnybrook black soil and the Cromwellian figure of the Manor.

Now as Bowman and Carter embarked on sprouts from the hills, Harry came over one Saturday to Fred Bushell's delight and planted a couple of rows of asparagus roots in the Manor garden and pruned the plum trees.

Down in the Thurness, a field Bowman and Carter rented from the Manor, Jack Gardener and Alf Miller were picking the late February sprouts with old Durgin Green.

' 'Tis a queer sort of name for a field, be you sure it yunt Furness, Master Bowman?' Alf Miller asked Tom as he carried a forty pound hamper of sprouts to the wooden tripod where the spring balances swung from a broken plough trace to weigh the vegetables for market.

'Funny you should say that, Alf, because Fred Bushell spread his field map on the kitchen table the other night and he told me the meaning of some of the field names. Thur comes from Thor, a giant, and Ness means a nose, so here is a giant nose. Couldn't describe it better I know, because when we marked the ground out for the plants in rows three feet apart we found the land tapered like a nose towards the Needle Lands. Now the name of those two fields speaks for itself, 'cos they be shaped long and narrow like a couple of needles. But do you remember Harry Carter and me working that heavy clay at Donnybrook called the Klondike? A sense of humour someone had, because there's been no gold rush there.'

Alf Miller had worked for Bowman and Carter since leaving the Blue Coat School. Before he married his wife Ida, and came to live in the village, he'd lived with his widowed mother in Nailer's Row amongst the nailers, those hard-working folk who scratched a living making the nails for a merchant on whose wharf on the Avon river the iron was shipped and the nails consigned to the trade. The leather-aproned men and their wives stood hammering the red hot metal into nails as their fathers had done.

Alf knew what poverty meant until the thirteenth birthday when he started work. From then on his employers, apart from paying him ten shillings a week, had fed him at dinner time on their bacon and eggs and Tom's mother's home baked bread. But now Alf had grown into a tall, useful young man earning sixteen shillings a week. Gone were the days of more meal times than meals and when he took a ticket from the parson to the bakers in Sheep's Heads Alley to buy a small loaf.

'My boy,' the baker had said, 'if the parson can afford a penny ha'penny I'll do the same. Take two loaves.'

Alf now in 1911 supported his mother who cleaned and scrubbed the riverside houses near Evesham bridge. Old Mrs. Miller fattened a pig in the little corrugated iron sty up the garden. A pig was greased at the Whitsuntide Fair to be caught as it ran the gauntlet between the Donnybrook women. Alf's mother, small, grey and spare, was lissom. She had caught up with the pig, held it, and won the prize.

'Can we afford to keep it Alf?' she'd asked her son. He answered with his usual laugh as he twirled his moustache and waxed it for church on Sunday, 'Keep it mother, of course, and it ull keep we later on. I'll buy some meal off Fred Bushell and bring it home on Harry Carter's dray.'

Alongside Alf in Thurness that February worked Jack Gardener, who lived at Donnybrook with his young wife. Before coming to Bowman and Carter Jack had learnt gardening from an old man in Pershore. His first job was turning the grindstone for his employer to sharpen the cabbage cutting knives. Then he followed his boss as the plum grafts were tied on to the plum tree stocks. He smoothed each joint with a gluey mixture of blue clay, cow muck and straw, like a plumber runs the lead around a water pipe, studying all the time the way the grafter made the union between the common root stock and the budded shoot of a desirable variety of plum with his sharp knife and raffia.

Jack rode with Min the nag in Harry Carter's dray every morning at six o'clock, winter and summer to under Bredon. The loaded dray of vegetables and fruit left the land under Bredon at five thirty in the evening with Jack for either the market or the station in Evesham town. Jack wore for work an Army uniform discarded by his soldier brother when he was demobbed after the Boer War. He himself was a smart young man, not very tall, but strong. 'A bit roguish,' Harry Carter described him. Being the youngest of a large family he had never experienced the shortage of food like Alf.

His father kept a pig at Pershore in a garden behind a terraced house with only one door. Jack described how all the pig food was carried through the passage or the hall to the back and the pig manure had to pass through from the garden to the road.

'A good system we had in Persha, Master Bowman. We got together and formed a sort of club so that we was utting pig mate for about seven wicks over the winter. No feast and a fast when all the offal, the spareribs and griskins was ut all in a feow days afore the mate went bad. I know chines can be salted down for christening parties, but I relishes my fittle fresh. The drill was if I killed my pig this wick, I ud shell the offal between seven neighbours and the buoys would deliver the mate to seven houses. Next wick another bloke kills iss'n, then we gets a morsel of his offal and so on for seven wicks. That tided the time from Christmas until after Valentine's Day.'

Tom Bowman listened to Jack's story with interest, being the youngest of thirteen children, he also never knew what it was to be hungry when the sisters brought home the scraps from the big houses where they worked in service when he was a boy.

Alf and Jack were two men who had learnt the art and mystery of market gardening from Harry Carter. He had insisted from the start that they bent their backs and drew the hoe blade until it almost touched the toe caps of their boots, then all the weeds were cut by what Harry called the hoove. Every plant was firmed by the setting pin and tested by pulling at the leaf with finger and thumb to prove when the leaf tore away that the plant was firm in the soil. So to pick thirty pots of sprouts in a day or plant five thousand cabbage plants was an ordinary work day in the lives of Alf and Jack.

' 'Twill be like a job in the town working on Bredon,' Alf told Tom Bowman. 'The clay in Thurness sticks to yer hummucks or yer fit kind of loving. On Bredon Hill if it rains from shut-eye till breakfast time that brashy soil won't pick up on yer fit.'

Tom Bowman knew that Harry's men were dab hands with the long net catching rabbits and that Fred Bushell would welcome a reduction in their numbers as the bussocks, as Alf called them, did graze the sparse grass keep on the hill. 'As long as you leave the pheasants and partridges alone,' Tom said, 'Mr. Bushell has given permission for you to net the rabbits.'

'Udn't touch a long tailed un, pretty they be with the gold, green and white collars above the brown feathers, but mind ya, Master Bowman, it has been known for a squat covey of partridges getting into the rabbit net at night time,' Alf said.

'If that happens you take the birds to Fred Bushell,' Tom answered with a worried look on his face.

Up on the hill on Valentine's Day, Bowman and Carter were ferreting the few rabbits out of Great Hill quarry. Harry's big fitcher ferret, a beautiful animal, piebald and keen was spouting up three rabbits under a great limestone rock on the quarry face, Tom lay stretched out on the grass with his ear close to the earth listening to the traffic underground. The rabbit the liner ferret was attacking was kicking his hind feet against the vicious animal who, with collar and line, had entered and chased his prey fifteen feet into the rock where the rabbits had tunnelled their passages and caverns.

'The bolt hole is over where Jim's scratching, Tom,' Harry said quietly as his forefinger and thumb held the ferret line and the fitcher every time he jumped pulled the line through Harry's hand like a hooked trout will snatch and spin the reel on a fisherman's rod.

Jim dived into the hole he had opened under the gorse, pulling a rabbit on to the grassy bank. 'Good dog, good dog,' Tom said as he took the rabbit from Jim's mouth and killed it.

'Fancy a shot, Tom, you haven't had one today? Come here, Jim, we'll let the next fella bolt.'

Tom stood with his gun cocked while Jim sat by Harry. Across the bottom of the quarry the rabbit bolted towards a patch of nettles. At thirty yards Tom emptied the cartridge of his twelve bore and before the noise of the gun had echoed among the limestone, the rabbit had pitch-poled to its death with lead shot between its long silky ears. 'Fetch him, Jim,' Harry spoke to his dog as man to man. 'Bring him here, boy,' he called as Jim picked up the rabbit.

Harry listening now to the bumping of feet underground closed the bolt hole for a while with a stone. 'More to come but the rabbit you shot Tom is a doe, heavy in kindle, quite milky. Dare say Mr. Harding won't be buying many more this spring.'

'They'll buy them in Birmingham. I'll send a wire to Mr. Fuller for some rabbit hampers, then we can rail some at the station,' Tom replied.

'What at about eight pence a piece,' Harry said with a laugh.

'There's no taste nor smell to nothing, Harry, and eight pence is better than nothing,' Tom answered to his senior partner.

'I'll tell you what it is though, Tom, I reckon it's a mistake to deal too much in little things. It's true the money mounts up, but if you deal in calves you are a calf all your life.'

'Going to get the graft and dig um out now,' Tom replied to Harry. 'It's getting on for four o'clock. The line's tight, the ferret has no doubt killed one rabbit and spouted the others up. I'll put a purse net over the bolt hole and maybe the live rabbit will bolt. I can't dig through rock.'

Lifting the stone from against the hole, Harry looked down among the rock and saw the grey fur of a rabbit two feet inside. He slipped his bared arm into the hole and pulled out one of the furry creatures referred to in Proverbs: 'The conies are but a feeble folk, yet make they their houses in the rocks.' No need now to use the purse net as the next rabbit, bitten badly by the ferret, came into Harry's hands. With snatches the loose line disappeared down the hole and Harry's ferret followed its prey, popping out through the bolt hole.

'That ull do for one day,' was Harry's remark as he put the rabbits into a potato sack, shouldered his double barrelled gun and walked beside Tom towards the barn.

As they reached the barn, the clump of trees alongside the old cattle yard were swaying in the wind. The bare beeches looked almost black in February while the row of fir trees towards Cobblers Quar bent their elastic branches, dipping the lower boughs, green as a desert oasis, almost to the ground. Bert Chandler appeared on the skyline riding his shaggy pony towards the cart track. He hailed Tom and Harry from the bridle gate. 'Ave ya caught the last rabbit on Bredon, me bwoys? Like squith they be. Leave a piece with two ends and that ull multiply.'

'Like a rabbit for yourself, Master Chandler?' Harry replied to the old man at the same time taking one from the sack and cracking its jaws together to make sure it was a young one.

'I see you know how to pick a young rabbit then, young Master Carter,' Bert Chandler said as he took the rabbit off Harry.

'Bit fresh up here, int it?' Tom Bowman remarked to the shepherd on horseback.

'Lazy wind, you, but we got March to come yet. Never come March, never come winter, and that's the blackthorn winter and the yow eaning snow.'

'Retires next year don't ya, Bert?' Harry said thinking what years of experience were wrapped up under the earth-coloured clothes the shepherd of the Manor wore. His hat was once a fur felt trilby belonging to one of Fred Bushell's visitors. Now it was weather beaten, the hatband faded. Over his cord trousers, broad falls, or fall fronts, his cord waistcoat had four pockets which held his tobacco, his turnip watch and this two pocket knives; one a bone handled shut knife to cut his bread and cheese bait, the other a sharp smaller one with 'Lambs Foot' stamped on the blade, which he used to pare the sheep's feet. Over all his clothes, reaching down to the top of his gaiters, Bert wore this kind of pinafore frock made of sacking tied at the waist with binder twine. This gave him a look like Moses or the prophets, or perhaps some ancient monk riding around the monastic farm land.

'Retiring,' he replied to Harry, 'spose I be. I'm trying to teach young Ruby, the gaffer's son, how to deal with the yows when they ean. Gaffer says he'd like me to keep an eye on the ship lambing time, shearing time and the like, but apart from that I'll have to live on the Lloyd George. Course we'll manage, the missus and me, and 'tis no secret I've put a bit by.'

'Goodish horse you have there,' Tom Bowman ventured.

'Oi Tom boy, 'tis a mare a course. Name of Violet. Her do take me up yer around the turnip field and I can put on a cart and haul a feow mangolds or a bit of hay. Then every wick me and Ruby hooks her unto the hoss gear as turns the chaff cutter. In the autumn her ull do the circuit again and turn the cider mill. Young Ruby drives her at hoss rake at haymaking. Unt bad, is it?' Bert Chandler said with a laugh. 'Come on now, girl, get me back to Ayshon and my tay.'

The men parted. Harry called after the shepherd, 'I wanted to ask you a favour, Bert.' As the mare stood another minute Harry explained that he and Tom Bowman were taking more land off Mr. Bushell and needed a horse team as they only had their two nags. Tom spoke up and said, 'The point is, could you come with us to the horse fair at Stow and choose some useful workers, if Mr. Bushell will give you the time off?'

'You buy the *Aysum Journal* and look out for a farm sale and I'll come along. Then we can buy horses, harness collars, mullins, all to fit and you don't want left-'anded hosses from the hoss fair, but tried and tested workers from a good farm.'

'Thank you,' the partners replied speaking as one man.

'Another thing, do you chaps play cricket?' Bert Chandler asked. ' 'Cos we got a meeting at the school to start a team. 'Tis Ruby's idea and I have stood umpire for matches at Dumbleton for years so I be interested.'

Tom replied, 'I'll play sometimes when we are not busy. Anyway I'll join the club.'

Harry took a golden sovereign from his pocket saying, 'Here put this towards the funds, but we'll come to the meeting.'

'Generous on ya, young sir. I'll see Mr. Bushell and get a receipt.'

At the White Hart that evening old shepherd Chandler found Ruby Bushell pinning a notice up in Singer Sallis' bar about the proposed cricket team. Tustin Finch, that somewhat gormless cattle man of Fred Bushell's, was bragging to Ruby how fast he could bowl. Bert Chandler looked across the bar, aimed at the spittoon and spat, disgusted that Tustin should be in such a state of liquor in front of the master's son.

'Talks as your belly guides ya,' Bert said, and taking a deep breath and drawing at his clay pipe, he added, 'thee hast got more to say than thee hast got to ett.'

Ruby put his hand on Bert's shoulder and said, 'Look here, Bert, encourage young Tustin. I know he's had a few pints but we want him in the team.'

'Only wish I hadn't sin so many Christmas days Ruby, and I'd spreadeagle the wickets a damn sight better than he,' Bert answered.

'I made fifty runs in a match last year,' Tustin said. 'What dost think a that, then you?'

'Not a lot,' Bert answered, ' 'cos I specks twas against the Blind School from Ooster.'

'Now, let's get off to a good start,' Ruby said, handing two pints of Singer Sallis' best beer to his men. So at the village school later that February night in 1911 the men of Ayshon met to form a cricket club. The neighbouring villages had been running teams for some years now but here it was not until the new curate of St. Barbara's came that a club was planned.

The Minute Book states that:

Meeting held at School, February 28th, 1911.
Present Rev. E. F. Rushton, Mr. F. Bushell, R. Bushell, B. Chandler, H. Carter, T. Finch, S. Sallis, T. Bowman, C. Jones, J. Hunt and Master Adam Hunt and Arthur Jackson, farmer from the Wood.
Rev. E. F. Rushton was elected Chairman.
Singer Sallis: Secretary.
Rev. Rushton: Captain.
Singer Sallis: Vice-Captain.
Ruby Bushell: Treasurer.
Frank Bishop: President, farmer from Broadenham.
It was proposed that the rules be drawn up and brought before the meeting.
Rule 1 The Club to be called Ayshon Cricket Club and shall be governed by the President and five Committee members with officers and ex officio members.
Rule 2 That each playing member shall pay one shilling per year.
Rule 3 That all new members be proposed and seconded at a Committee meeting by members of the Club.

Rule 4 That the eleven members to play in matches shall be picked by the Committee on the Monday before the match and each member shall give notice to the Committee on the Wednesday following if he is unable to play.

Rule 5 That practice nights be Mondays, Wednesdays and Fridays.

Rule 6 That the cricket things shall not be taken out without the presence of a member.

Rule 7 That the Committee reserve the right to dismiss any member for disorderly or bad conduct on the field.

Edgar Rushton
Chairman.

So it was on the last day of February the Cricket Club was formed. It seemed to put new life into Bert Chandler who looked forward to being their umpire. He talked to Tustin Finch in the barn as they cut the chaff one wet day, emphasising to him the importance of the team spirit and not to be so big-headed about his bowling.

'When we play Dumbleton I can name at least three batsmen there who ull knock sixes off thee.'

Fred Bushell came along and listened to the men, then told Tustin that Bert was handy with the ball years ago and respected all around the hill. The rain pattered down on the roof of the dutch barn and Bert took four or five strides towards the bay full of hay and brought his arm over with an imaginary ball, as he had done years ago.

'He would bowl you out today, Tustin,' Fred Bushell said with a laugh.

'Got a bat and ball, sir?' Bert asked.

'Young Ruby's got one in the dairy. I'll fetch it.'

As Fred reappeared with bat and ball, Bert Chandler stuck three rick pegs in the ground up against the bay of hay. 'It yunt a chain long Tustin, but thee get hold of that bat and I'll show ya.' Bert put a steady ball down on the barn floor, pitching wide of the off stump it came in and knocked the stump down. Fred laughed. In fact they all laughed at Bert bowling a break ball to Tustin six months short of his seventieth birthday.

'Now we'll get on with the chaff cutting, Gaffer,' Bert said. 'What about putting some of the hay with the straw to cut for my yows?'

'Do that Bert. 'Tis a bit mouldy, not harvested very well.'

Tustin added, 'Oi, the store cattle in the Cinder Meada be a bit choice over eating it when the mornings be open.'

'They ud sooner eat that than their fore feet or a snowball, I'll warrant,' Bert answered.

So farmer Bushell's work was done, always if possible, ahead of his neighbours. In the barn the notice read, 'A place for everything and everything in its place.' 'Remember that, Tustin,' the shepherd said, 'and don't do what tha did when tha was a bwoy and come to me and say, "Anybody seen a shovel, 'cos there's one in the barn missing." '

'You'll do, Tustin,' Fred Bushell said. 'But remember when I asked you why you never came to work one day and you replied, "Oi, Master, I stopped at home and went on the train to Aysum." ' Tustin went redder and redder knowing that his elders were speaking the truth.

3

Lady Day

THE 25TH MARCH WAS RENT DAY, THE SEASON OF GREAT
rent dinners supplied by landlords. Fox cubs are reckoned to be born
on Lady Day, Caring Sunday, the Sunday before Palm Sunday,
known also as Passion Sunday.

'Never come March, never come winter,' Bert Chandler called
out to Tustin Finch as he carried a stack of withy hurdles on his back
across the yard of the Manor Cross Barn.

' 'Tis the yow eaning snow, Bert, and thee just look how kind the
blackthorn hedge shows up in its white blow anant the road.'

'Oi, allus a bad month, you,' Bert replied.

Tom was making some more burra hurdles, thatched with straw
to shelter his late lambs from the driving snow. The snow whiffled
over the short early grass in the cider orchard, leaving some places on
top of the high ridged lands quite free and still showing that early
green so welcome in March. Little drifts formed under the blackthorn hedge, but Bert looked at the break in the clouds, saw the weak
sun and laughed, looked at Rosie his dog and said, ' 'Twill be
different tomorrow.'

Tustin Finch ambled across the yard to the old shepherd and sure
enough the sun shone and the snow dripped wet off the orchard
trees, the little drift under the blackthorn turned to slush, the older
lambs came from their shelter near the burra hurdles and raced like
children around the orchard.

'Wants to cut them this wick, happen,' Bert said to Tustin as thirty
strong lambs ran by, dodging among the trees.

'Cruel job I reckon, Bert, drawing their stones and cutting their
tails with a knife. Never aught to be allowed. You udn't like to be
served like that, ud ya?'

Bert, pulling his clay pipe from his mouth spat towards the

nearest apple tree then said, 'Every damn year as comes along some
silly devil like thee interferes with my work. It ud be a blessing if thee
was cut for the simples, then ya udn't be so keen biking over to
Tewkesbury wenching. I'd see that no girl belonging to me was ever
in the same turnip field as thee. Now just slope off and trouble tha
yud of tha own interference.'

As the shepherd and cowman spoke Fred Bushell opened the yard
gate with his riding cane and rode towards his men.

'Morning, Bert, it looks a little brighter. The snow never lasts long
in March, you know.'

'Yes, sir. I reckon it's about over for this year. Mind there's still
some on top of Bredon.'

'Waiting for some more,' Tustin butted in.

'Just bin telling Tustin here that what he knows and what he don't
know amounts to a hell of a lot.'

Tustin, who was carrying his hay fork, leant on it, then pointed
towards Winchcombe, 'Still black over our Bill's Mother's,' he said
in a sneering sort of way.

'Now where could that be,' Mr. Bushell asked.

'Winchcombe Hole and it allus rains or snows when the sun gets
down, along of the wind,' Tustin replied.

As the lambs careered around in the spring sunshine, Fred Bushell
turned to his shepherd saying, 'Bert, if it's a decent morning
tomorrow I'll send young Adam and Ruby to help you cut the
lambs.'

Bert nodded in agreement. Tustin sniggered and Fred was
annoyed. Waving his cane he said, 'Have you finished work for
today because ya know there's that hedge to layer in Calve's Gore.'

'I've foddered all the cattle and cleaned out the calf pens and 'tis my
bait time,' Tustin replied.

As Tustin walked away Bert said in a whisper to his master, 'Bin
on about me being cruel castrating the lambs with my front teeth.'

'Take no notice, Tustin's about three ha'pence short of a shilling,
but he's strong and looks after the cattle pretty well.'

Bert looked up at Fred Bushell on his cob. 'Might be as well if
Ruby cut a few lambs tomorrow as I shan't be amongst it next year?'

'Ah Bert, he talks about using the bloodless castrators next year.'

Bert Chandler spat on the ground among the strawy pen, walked away from the cob, then returned. Thinking aloud, he said, 'Blood-less,' then said, 'You know sir, my method have been used since before the remembrance of man.'

Next morning Adam met the shepherd and the young gaffer, Ruby Bushell, in the Cross Barn. The ewes and lambs were in hurdle pens. The men and the boy lifted the lambs over the hurdles into a pen of their own. Bert Chandler whetted his bone handled shut knife then dressed himself in his herden overall tying some binder twine around his waist as a belt. A bucket of water stood by the door and on a shelf next to his pipe and costrel of cider was a packet of twist tobacco which Mr. Bushell had provided.

'Now bwoy,' Bert told Adam, 'if it's a yow lamb just hold it still for me to dock it on the ground, but the young tups ya'll hold by the four legs against your shoulder with your back against the door post. Catch one, Ruby, and show him, ull ya.'

Ruby caught a tup lamb and held it as Bert explained, then gave it to young Adam. With his knife Bert took about an inch off the young lamb's purse, then leaning towards it he grasped one testicle in his teeth and pulled until the cord broke. He dropped the sweet-bread into the water then drew the other stone. The lamb winced a little throwing its head against Adam's chin. The twist tobacco was constantly being chewed by Bert's few remaining teeth, and he spat some of the tobacco juice first into one cavity where the testicle had been and then into the other.

'Stand him down, bwoy,' he ordered Adam and with his knife he tailed the lamb who staggered a little shaken back to the pen.

Adam looked up at the shepherd and was shocked to see the old man's moustache so stained with brown twist tobacco and the blood of a young lamb. 'Allus bin the same since Adam was a bwoy,' the old man muttered.

Down on the clayland of the Butts, a field which often grew forty tons of mangolds to the acre after a dressing of well rotted manure from the yards, the winter wheat was growing green, recovering from the winter weather. Fred Bushell sent Tustin and Jones the under carter to hoe between the rows of corn. The frost had left a nice sugary mould or tilth, and the rows of wheat were now tall enough to hide a hare.

'It's a fifteen acre ground and I'll pay you by the acre,' Fred told his men.

As their hoe blades cut the chickweed, the early thistles and docks, Tustin told Jones of how men got their money by hoeing one row and scuffing another row with their heavy hob-nailed boots. 'And another thing,' he said, 'some men just hoe the outside of the field and a piece by the gate and the gaffer doesn't often walk to the centre of the crop.'

'Dost reckon thee bist man enough to fool our gaffer like that, 'cos if I know Fred Bushell he ull walk this field afore he pays us for the work. No, Fred Bushell knows how many beans make five,' Jones added.

'A nice field of wheat over the hedge in Mr. Jim Cambridge's field, you,' Tustin remarked, 'but what be the telegraph wires for, I wonder?'

'They be growing wheat by 'lectric so I heard Singer Sallis say in the pub. A man from Staffordshire Mr. Cambridge is and a long-headed un, so they say.'

'There's a couple of fellows hoeing over there and the wheat looks kind. I'll go and have a look at bait time.'

'Trouble with you, Tustin, you won't mind your own business. What if Mr. Cambridge comes?'

At lunch time Tustin bolted his bread and cheese, then climbed the fence into the next field. Two men were hoeing up and down under the wires which were stretched about ten feet above the ground from pole to pole.

'I know you chaps, you travel to Worcester on Saturdays, and come back on the Drunken Willy train at eleven o'clock, the one that Jones and I came back on when I bought my boots from a shop in the Shambles.'

'That's right, but be careful in this field 'cos the big generators be pumping electric current along these wires and you'd get a hell of a shock if you touched them,' a tall thin man from Pershore replied.

'Unt no danger as I can see when I seen the starlings perched up in rows,' Tustin replied. 'Lend us your hoe and I'll prove it,' he added and he stood with the hoe in the air until he touched a wire. Tustin fell forward loosing the hoe stale. Mr. Cambridge's men grabbed him and sat him up among the rows of wheat.

'Silly sod,' one said, 'won't be told, will ya!'

But Bushell's cowman insisted that one of the men had hit him behind his legs. 'Get back to thee own field and in future don't meddle with up to date corn growing,' was the parting shot from Cambridge's men.

When young Adam heard of what happened to Tustin he kept clear of Cambridge's wheat field, but looked over the fence and did reckon that the crop was better than any of Mr. Bushell's.

Fred Bushell was never a hunting man, not because he objected to it—he allowed the Croome pack to hunt on his land—but Fred started life the hard way when he was a boy, tied to a cow's tail, he said, with very little let up for sport, apart from what fell to his gun. Young Ruby followed the pack when they met in the village, but was never allowed more than two or three days a week in the chase.

A footpath to Parson's Folly on Bredon summit went alongside and linked the hill land and Holcombe Nap with an ash coppice where the violets and primroses showed cream and purple among the other greenery, ground ivy and kingcups wreathing the ash and sally stools.

John Hunt, Adam's father was the official earth stopper on the eastern side of Bredon. In the darkness of a March morning he stopped the holes shutting out the foxes after their nightly hunt for rabbits on the hill. The fox earth in the ash coppice had been reynard's home, the birth place of cubs, for years.

Like the track of the badger which he follows in a run year after year, leaving the tell-tale strands of grey hair on barbed wire along the side of a ditch, so the fox earth is almost a permanant thing, immovable. As the badger pads his run and works his way into open country from his set under the fence or hedge which steals a little of his coat, so the fox burrows deep into the rock of the hill, leaving a bevy of soil at his doorway. John Hunt stopped the earth in the ash coppice.

The hounds met at the White Hart that March morning and after drawing Ayshon wood, they took the fox to Grafton Firs where they lost him. From Grafton coppice another fox was hallowed by Bert Chandler as it crossed Quar Hill towards the Cuckoo Pen. This proved to be a vixen making for the ash coppice.

Fred Bushell, riding his cob across Holcombe Nap where some outlying store cattle were being fed by young Adam, sensed that a vixen had whelped some cubs in the earth in his coppice. As the music of the pack got nearer a tired vixen passed his cob and tried to get to ground in the earth. Fred tied his horse to an elder tree and shouted to Adam, 'Here boy, quick! Over that fence into the coppice and unstop that earth.'

Fred gave the boy a leg over the larch fence and in no time at all Adam moved the board from the mouth of the hole, stood back a few yards among the brambles and saw the vixen return to her young. The ash coppice grew on a steep bank towards a stream at Shaw Green and before Adam could retrace his tracks to the field fence, the hounds bore upon him taking him off his feet and pitchpolling him to the bottom.

'Good lad," Fred Bushell said. 'I didn't want those cubs to be motherless.'

When the huntsman arrived Fred explained to him the unstopped earth. 'Lady Day the cubs are usually born, but this vixen had an early litter.'

'Hunting's about over for this year, sir,' the huntsman admitted as the two men rode side by side down Cotton's Lane. What a contrast the two made, hunting pink and a sleek hunter, tweeds and box hat and a shaggy cob.

That Friday, after Durgin's wife Annie had prepared a meal for this broad shouldered Cromwellian figure he sat under the ingle with young Ruby and read the local weekly *Journal*. Annie looked after the Bushell household after Fred had been left a widower. Friday night after Fred had paid his men he usually smoked a pipe and shared a bottle of wine with Ruby and sometimes the vicar.

'Winchcombe court had a busy day this week,' Fred announced to his son. 'I see where two chaps Thomas Phillip and John Core were each fined six pence for leaving their horses unattended outside the Corner Cupboard Inn. Wet through they said they were on the road back from Stratford with a load of cattle cake on the waggon.'

'A bit much,' Ruby replied, 'picking on farm chaps like that. No doubt the horses would stand a bit, while they had a pint.'

' 'Tis against the law Ruby, and that must be kept. I remember when Will Archer was fined one shilling for his donkey straying, must be fifteen year ago now,' Fred replied. He read on. 'I see the chauffeur from Guiting Grange was fined five shillings for having no tail light on the car. He said he lit it twice and twice it went out. And some boys were summoned for playing football on a Sunday, but the vicar spoke for them and the case was dismissed.' On another page there was coverage of the Gloucester Show.

'Got the judges' remarks here Ruby, when they walked the fields.' "We would like to see more vetches grow but with one or two exceptions the tenants are trying to improve the farms. The rick-yards are tidy and better kept. The corn and hayricks do not present such a neglected appearance as before. Hedge cutting is going apace, but the hedge layer is absent the day of reckoning will come.' On the whatnot in the Bushell's sitting room was a silver tea service pre-sented to him by a landlord for good farming on a farm he had rented from a neighbouring estate. Turning to his son, Fred then said, 'That reminds me, how's Tustin getting on with our hedge layering?'

'Finished for this year Dad, 'tis the 25th March.'

'So it is. Ah, here's a bit about Ayshon. Mr. A. Holyoak has written in the paper to say that the roadman's ill and the roads are a disgrace. There's water running down the village street, the brook's full of filth and Carrants Brook should be a thing of beauty. Com-pare this with Dumbleton, Overbury or Beckford. What is our Councillor doing? If he can't get justice done let him give place to one who will. Nasty knock at Doctor Overthrow that is, Ruby. Been our Councillor now for eleven years. Perhaps he'll get things done now he's just been made Chairman of the Pebworth R.D.C.'

'Roadmen are known to be slow workers, Dad. Bert Chandler told me that if you could catch a drop of sweat off a roadman that would kill a toad.'

'Don't forget, Ruby my boy, our roadman who's ill has been one of the best. It doesn't pay to generalise. But never mind about our roads now. The doctor 'll take care of them. For one thing he uses the Groaten down to the station as much as anyone with that lissom horse, Lavender, and the trap when he catches the Evesham train.'

'Catches it,' Ruby laughed. 'He's always late and complaining that the station clock is fast, and many's the time when he goes to

Cheltenham they stop the train along the line by the goods siding and the old man gets in the carriage there.'

'Never gets to bed until after midnight,' Fred replied. 'He reckons never to go for his rest until all the rogues and vagabonds are in bed.'

'Fair play, Dad, he's always on call every night. He had to stitch Tustin Finch's mother up the other night. She's a big woman, Dad, as you know, and the chamber pot collapsed under her when she sat on it in the bedroom and the jagged piece cut her pretty bad.'

'Ah, a man and a half, our doctor is, and the working man can't afford to pay him. I remember the time when Bert Chandler's mother was touch and go with pneumonia. 'Twas on a Sunday night and he was out of linseed for poultices and Bert started up my Rushton and Honsby oil engine with a blow lamp by the light of a lantern, and he and the doctor ground some of my linseed into meal for a poultice. Bert's Dad belonged to the Cirencester Club so the doctor got a little pay for that. But damn it, Ruby, it's eleven o'clock and it's bedtime, well very near the doctor's bedtime, and I want you to start Jones and Adam drilling oats in the morning up behind Grafton Firs. Jones dressed the seed today, I hope, with the vitriol.' Ruby nodded, finished his drink, and went to bed.

He tossed and turned a while, but sleep seemed far away. Was this Elizabethan Manor house with eight bedrooms, attics and cellars really haunted? Bert Chandler often talked of the time it was exorcized by the Bishop many years ago. He said a human skeleton was found behind the panelling in the great hall and sounds were heard at night which could not be explained. Ruby jumped out of bed when he heard a knocking noise by the dairy. From his window in the moonlight orchard he saw old Merriman, the heavy shire horse, kicking his heels against a cow crib. 'Bit of grease no doubt under the feather of his hooves,' he thought. 'I'll have to dress that with Stockholm tar tomorrow.' He got back into bed, blew out the candle.

Next day in the big barn Jones and Adam stood in the half light of morning. On the old threshing floor where Bert Chandler's Dad had used the flail to thresh the corn years ago a heap of seed oats lay ready for sacking. The huge double doors at each side of the barn were wide open to let in the bit of light there was.

'That's a rum un,' Jones said to Adam, 'a cross has been made on top of the heap.'

Ruby was joined by old Bert Chandler who was chuckling to himself. 'What's this cross here?' Adam asked Bert.

'That's put there to keep the divil away. Always the sign of the cross bwoy, and you chaps neglected to do that, so when I came into the barn last night with my lantern, I made one. Always keep on the right side of old Nick is my maxim.'

'I see,' Adam replied. 'Is that a fact Mr. Bushell?'

'Yes,' Ruby said, 'now hold the mouth of the sacks and Jones'll fill them. They be only a hundred and a half weight, Adam, you can carry one off the cart when we get on the hill.'

With Merriman and Noble the man and boy took a cartload of seed up Bredon. 'We'll put Merriman in the shafts and you lead Noble in front,' Jones said, 'but Ruby is coming along presently to set the new Knap drill to put on a sack to the acre.'

It was the first time young Adam had carried a sack, so he was pleased to put his shoulders under one hundred weight and a half and be as good a man as Jones. After Ruby had set the drill and the horses had done several bouts backwards and forwards behind the Firs, Bert Chandler arrived on his pony.

'The gaffer says you are to drill some sainfoin seed crossways the oats when you have finished,' he told Jones. 'Now there's a useful crop to grow some fodder for the yows, as beautiful a flower the red blow is as ever growed in anyone's garden. Ah,' he added, 'I suppose I'll be drawing the Lloyd George when that's ready to harvest.'

Over by Great Hill Barn in the fifteen acre where Tom Bowman and Harry Carter were to plant the sprouts, Durgin Green was working. Although Mr. Carter had thinned out the rabbits in the nearby quarry there was still a sprinkling of them left. Craven's of Evesham were manufacturing a product known as Rabbit Smear, or animal oil. It was a good repellant to keep rabbits away from vegetable crops, to keep foxes away from pheasant nests, a vile smelling brown liquid sold in cans. Bowman and Carter bought a quantity of this smear and sent Durgin up the hill to apply it.

The method was to soak binder twine in the animal oil and with sticks like rick pegs to circle the headland of the prospective crop with a strand of the string soaked in the oil fixed to the pegs so that it was about twelve inches off the ground. It really worked, but poor Durgin had an unenviable task applying it.

Tustin Finch was foddering the outlying bullocks on Spring Hill and he and Adam and Jones met in the barn to eat their bait. Durgin came through the door and as he passed Tustin sitting on an upturned hamper Tustin held his nose.

'Hast thee stepped in summat, Master Green, or as summat crawled up inside ya? You stinks like a fitcher ferret.'

'Now they do say that foxes smells their own scent, perhaps it's you that stinks.' Tustin looked to Jones and Adam for support, but they kept quiet. 'What's this I hear about Bert Chandler trying to keep away the devil out of the oats?'

'It's an old custon,' Adam replied, 'and I'm not going to dispute it.'

'The sign of the cross, I don't know.'

'I suppose you be gwain to argue about all the customs that our fathers have handed down then, Tustin Finch.'

'Such as what,' he replied.

Durgin then went on to tell the three in the barn what he believed in. 'I'm not a religious sort of chap, but the laying of the ghost at the Manor by the Bishop, I believe in.' Durgin, like Bert Chandler had been reared on a mixture of the superstitions of old Gloucestershire and the observations of their ancestors.

'I heard Mother say that a whistling woman and a crowing hen is neither good for God nor men,' Adam ventured, 'and Mr. Bushell does kill a hen if it crows and Mother doesn't like a woman to whistle.'

'That's true, bwoy,' Durgin replied, adding 'And I'd sooner go cold than burn elderberry wood.'

'For why?' Tustin said, with his silly smile.

'Cos the divil comes down the chimney if ya do,' Durgin replied.

'Now, Tustin, you are a single chap with little responsibility. Would you kill a pig when the moon was on the wane and risk the bacon frying away in the pan?' Jones said at last. 'I tell you a servant girl at Beckford handled some bacon curing in the salting lead when she had her monthly, and that all went bad.'

' 'Tis all my eye,' the cowman replied.

' 'Tis time we made a move,' Jones announced, 'and I suppose the oats we plant are one for the pigeon, one for the crow, one to rot, and the other to grow.'

'One thing I've always found to be true,' Durgin said, 'if you get a hot cross bun which is baked on Good Friday and keep that in the chimney corner, it's good for a youngster with the belly ache.'

'That's about the licker,' Tustin said as the workers left the barn.

'All right then,' was Durgin's parting shot, 'I'll be the bear and you be the pretty boy.'

Working for Bowman and Carter, Durgin was so often on his own in the fields. Jack Gardener and Alf Miller were the other men but being younger and more adaptable to Harry Carter's methods of working the land, they were apart from Durgin.

This little man who was breeched and gaitered in the winter wore trousers much too long for him, the waistband reaching almost to his armpits with very little shirt showing beneath his broad leather braces—braces he received as a prize at a flower show years ago. His arched eyebrows and a moustache which always appeared somewhat askew gave him a cynical appearance which was quite untrue. His wife, Annie, was a strong supporter at the chapel, an inexhaustable knitter and worker with the crochet hook. She made clothes for half the village children.

The fact that Jack Gardener's wife had three children and Alf Miller's wife had just given birth to twins upset Durgin. Tustin, that uncouth cowman of Bushell's had said to Alf before the twins were born, 'Expecting again then, you? Yer yunt empty for long. Couples pretty regular, don't ya?'

Durgin standing by, looked very annoyed. His moustache twitched, he cleared his throat and said nothing.

'Thee bisn't old enough to understand and if any poor ooman agreed to get hooked up with a crater like you I'd be sorry,' Alf replied. 'Marriage unt just stock breeding, you silly young oaf.'

Tustin leaned against a cart in the open cart shed; he made Durgin's blood boil. The fire was burning on the yard floor and the men had finished their bait after cooking their fat bacon on nut sticks over the flames. Tustin threw a crust on to the fire.

'If the Good Lord knew anything better then seck coupling, I mean, he kept it to himself.'

This remark of Tustin's stirred old Durgin, 'Remember the

Commandments,' he shouted, 'taking God's name in vain! A man could be struck dead for saying that. Another thing, that's downright wicked of you, burning bread on the bait-time fire. I hope you'll live to want.'

'Go hungry to closet,' Alf added with a smile.

After Tustin had gone back to the cattle yard, Alf Miller put his hand on little Durgin's shoulder and said, 'I never thought it was so easy to get a youngster. Come on Durgin, whatever be you and Annie messing at.'

Reverend Rushton, the vicar, visited Mrs. Ida Miller after the twins were born. After congratulating her and giving her the usual tin of cocoa as a present to encourage the yield of her milk, he took the coupon out of the tin, as he saved them, then said, 'You remember Psalm 128 used at your marriage service: "thy wife shall be as a fruitful vine upon the walls of thy house. Thy children like the olive branches round thy table." You have been faithful since then, but poor Durgin and Annie are still without children. Strange are God's ways.'

Ida smiled looking at her two youngest tucked in a bacon box asleep in the stone paved kitchen. ' 'Tis like this, Vicar. It's that early morning train on the branch line.'

'Now how can you put your, your . . . fertility down to a train, Ida?' he asked puzzled.

'Well, the banana train from Avonmouth runs rattling through Ayshon station at bout a quarter to five every morning and it's too early for Alf to get up and we dussunt go off to sleep again, so we couples, ya see.'

'Well, well, fancy a train being responsible for more names on the parish register in a few years time.'

The vicar stayed a few minutes, drank his tea, then left to see Annie Green, although Annie was an Irish Presbyterian and had attended the village chapel since she came to the village as a girl in domestic service.

'Many are called, but few are chosen,' he quoted to Annie who was so depressed.

'Barren I am, Vicar,' as if it was a sin, she replied.

A couple of years ago Annie Green had thought up a scheme in her thatched cottage by the walnut tree whereby she could show the village she was expecting. With feathers from an old bed, she packed herself a kind of pillow at bust and waist beneath her blouse and skirt. A little padding at first, then she had told Durgin she was expecting. As the weeks passed Annie put more padding under her clothes until Tustin called out from Bowman and Carter's cowyard, 'Thee hast managed that bit of a job at last, Durgin!'

Annie Green's figure became more rotund every week.

'When be ya going to be a Daddy?' Tustin asked Durgin. 'Annie looks close to profit.'

Durgin had looked over his allotment hedge at young Tustin Finch and could see that he had been too long at the White Hart. 'The drink's talking, or else you wouldn't speak to a fella like cattle are described in the market. If you must know, 'tis the end of the month.'

Poor Durgin was still deluded, and the following week Annie took the eight fifty train from the station to Evesham, changed on to the London line and boarded the train for Paddington. She told Durgin she was to have the child in a London nursing home run by the Salvation Army. A telegram came to Ayshon Midland Station that the baby was stillborn and had been a little lad. Durgin was upset, but was more upset when he later found out the truth. And, as Alf Miller said, she had been drawing a maternity benefit also known as the Lloyd George. This was refunded by Durgin's employers. On her return, Annie spent her time minding other women's babies while they worked on the land. A sad story about Annie who so wished to have a child and not disappoint Durgin. Durgin bought a liver and white spaniel called Tiny and that was the only baby they ever had.

The vicar didn't stay long with Annie Green, just leaving the parish magazine. At keeper Finch's house he was hailed by a bent old man, Tustin's father.

'Good morning, Keeper,' he said, 'I've just seen Alf Miller's twins.'

'Ah, daresay they be pleased,' Keeper replied, 'but of course all our nine children be married and away except young Tustin.'

'A creditable family you have,' was the vicar's comment.

'To be sure they be, but young Tustin's a gallus young devil. When I went to school, 'twas in St. Barbara's vestry then mind,

Reverend Joseph Harrison taught I that one and one made two. Damn it, when we had been married a few years one and one made nine, not two, as Parson said.'

'You will do, Keeper,' the vicar replied. 'I must be on my way. I'm having a game of cards, a pipe of tobacco and a drink with Mr. Bushell tonight.'

Durgin spent the next week hoeing the young sprout plants in Harry Carter's garden ready for the April planting. Harry Carter was secretive about his journeys up Bredon Hill.

'He's planting something,' Alf said to Durgin. 'He carried a rake and a bag of seed these past feow mornings.'

Harry knew what he was doing for he had purposely instructed Durgin to leave a patch of a quarter of an acre on the quarry side of the sprout field free from the animal oil fence of string. Here he planted parsley seed. Not to grow for market, but to entice all the hares on the hill to provide shooting for himself and Tom.

The hares had been plentiful this March and were left to their own desserts now, for neither the beagles nor the harriers hunted late in the season. The jack hares were as mad as March hares, as they are said to be. They follow the does miles in courtship. They box each other standing on their hind legs and if a pack of hounds were to chase a jack so late in the season he would take them a merry trip, running in a straight line and not in circles as he usually does when not mating. So Harry rubbed his hands as he looked over the wall and saw the antics of the hares. He thought, 'Ah, next November, when the sprouts are tall the hares will come and lie among the crop and feed off the quarter acre of parsley. Good practice for Tom and me with our twelve bores, good dinners too.' The old folk in Ayshon said March doesn't finish until the 12th April, a relic of the old pre-eighteenth-century calendar. Perhaps it was the March weather. However Bert Chandler's father always said when he talked of the hard winter of 1888, 'We had sixteen weeks frost in February. What a month!'

4

A Feast of Fools

While April morn her folly's throne exalts,
While Dob calls Nell and laughs because she halts,
While Nell meets Tom and says his tail is loose,
Then laughs in turn and calls poor Thomas goose,
Let as my Muse thro' folly's harvest range
And glean some moral into Wisdom's grange.
                                        1782

THE FIRST OF APRIL IS WELL KNOWN AS APRIL FOOLS DAY
or a Feast of Fools. It was observed in ancient Britain as the Feast of
the vernal equinox, a high and general festival in which unbounded
hilarity reigned. The sun at that period of the year enters the sign of
Aries. Rural sports and what was known as Vernal Delights were
supposed to begin. A widespread custom survives whereby every-
body tries to make as many fools as they can. In the country it often
meant sending folk on useless or what were called sleeveless errands,
for the history of Eve's mother, for pigeon's milk, hurdle seed or
strap oil. When a ploughboy went to the saddler on one of these
errands for strap oil, he received a few smacks on his breeches with a
breeching strap. Hunting the gowk or the cuckoo was another
pastime on the day.

Bert Chandler recalled that as a boy he was sent by the farmer with
a sack bag filled with something heavy to another farmer, often it
was clods of earth. The farmer, knowing the game sent him to the
next farmer, saying, 'It's not for me boy, but Farmer Jones.' Poor
Robin in his almanac of 1760 says, 'Which is the greatest fool, the boy
that went with the sack, or the farmer who sent him.'

April on the Manor Farm in 1911 was all go. The under carter,
Jones, and Adam had trouble in the stable with Merriman, Noble,

Prince, Pleasant and Blackbird. As the grass grew green under the hawthorn hedges, the horses trimmed the young shoots while at the manger they blew and snorted over the chaff, mangolds and oat flour. 'They be choice now, Adam, 'tis allus the same in April, finicky over their fittle.' Adam learnt that after the winter when the horses relied on the bait in the manger and the clover in the rack, they now spoilt their appetites on the new grass growing in sheltered spots in the sun.

Fred Bushell sent young Adam with Merriman to harrow the stale furrows of Finches Piece ready for planting the mangolds. Merriman had been a cavalry horse in the Boer War. Fred bought him off the War Department in 1904 as a seven-year-old. Now at fourteen he was a staid member of the Manor team. In the Army Merriman had learnt that when the order came to charge you responded.

As young Adam sauntered backwards and forwards across the furrows of Finches Piece, Tustin was behind the hedge in the perry orchard over the ditch where the withy trees were greening in the spring. 'Charge,' he shouted after Adam had turned his horse on the headland. Merriman leapt forward, snatching his traces tight in front of the whipple tree. Adam found that the rope G.O. reins slipped through his hands like the line on a hooked fish, but he held on while Merriman trotted with the harrows to the next headland.

On return, Tustin laughed over the hedge and said, 'That ull wake both on you up, bwoy. I had to get behind a pear tree before to see if ya were moving or standing still.'

'I'll tell Master Bushell of thee, Tustin. Merriman might have run away,' Adam said.

'Yer's a Woodbine, and don't thee say anything.'

With this, the cowman and ploughboy stood in the burra of the hedge and had a smoke.

Alf and Jack were working with Durgin cutting early spring cabbage in the Thurness field and packing them sixty pound in a hamper. Harry Carter's horse, Min, was drawing the hampers on a dray to the railway station. The heavy land had set bone hard after the rains; so dry it was that men, animals and the land itself was crying out for rain.

'We get just a scud,' Jack said to Alf, 'and the wind dries that little shower in less than an hour.' Mr. Carter's dray bumped and bounced over the concrete-like land.

Harry Carter drove his iron grey gelding along the Cheltenham road from his new house in Donnybrook. He walked among the cabbages then told the men not to waste one leaf of the green stuff. 'It's gold this spring, and once that's harvested there will be nothing without it rains.' He looked at the dried up spring onions and the blighted broad beans, then walked back to the roadside shed, put his foot on the step of his governess cart, and clicked his tongue for Dick, his cob, to start.

As they trotted up the Groaten road to Stanley Farm where Tom Bowman had recently gone to live, he thought that now they had buildings, a barn and a stable, it was time he and Tom bought a team of horses. Harry put Dick into a loose box at the end of the stable. He walked across the yard and opened the back door of the farm house. 'Tom,' he called, 'I've just come over from Evesham. How's the cabbage trade?'

'Flying trade at the moment, Harry. The merchants all eager to buy.' Tom was sitting at a big deal table in the kitchen. He had lit a fire in the oven grate and the kindling wood was still spitting as it burnt under the nuts of coal. A tin kettle swung on the pot hooks and was just on the boil. 'Cup of tea? My word, you are about early this morning.'

Harry watched Tom pour a cup of tea from the brown crock pot, then put the pot back on the hob to keep warm. On the table were invoices, bills, time sheets and a tinful of pea checks, those tin discs he and Harry gave to the pickers in the field to exchange at the court window for money. Tom was writing invoices and putting up the wages for the men.

'I was up at four o'clock this morning, Tom. Started from Evesham at six and was in the cabbage field as the men started work at half past.'

Tom smiled and nodded to his partner, knowing what a man he was for the morning. 'Ah, I'd got the furnace going for the washing at half past four and cooked the bacon at five. Got a gas cooker, haven't you, Harry, in your new house?'

'Yes, Tom, and gas lighting.'

Tom, who had never known such luxury gave the fire a **poke,** sending the sparks up the chimney, a chimney piece big enough to take a waggon and horses, then said, 'You know, Harry, you'll miss the gas and the flush lavatory when you come to live at the Lower Farm at Michaelmas.'

'But I'll be on top of Bredon Hill before it's light in the morning, that ull save that five mile drive from Evesham. I've told the men not to waste a leaf of those cabbages, Tom. What did Jim Carnow pay this week?'

'Seven and six a pot. That's money isn't it, Harry?'

'I'd say so,' Harry replied. 'When I think of cutting cabbage in Klondike for nine pence a pot a couple of years ago. But how about buying some horses, Tom, I'm getting fed up of being beholden to Fred Bushell to lend us one for drill or harrow when he says he's got one to spare. There's a farm sale advertised here over at Wormington next week.'

Thumbing the *Evesham Journal*, Tom Bowman showed Harry the advert. 'A big sale, Tom,' Harry went on, as he read, ' "Ninety-six cattle, half-bred Herefords, two hundred and seventy ewes and their lambs, seventeen horses viz. twelve cart horses, three-, four-, five-year-old and aged. The older horses have worked in all gears and the three-year-old in chains. Four cobs, quiet to ride and drive, and a child's pony." I reckon that's a better idea to go to the farm sale than go to Evesham, Stow or Pershore to the horse fairs. Bert suggested we could buy some trouble at a fair.'

'Bit of bread and cheese, Harry?' Tom said as he cut himself a piece of bread.

'Just a mouthful or two. It's a long while since I had breakfast,' Harry answered.

There was a knock at the front door and Tom walked the fifteen yards over the stone-slabbed hall and unbarred the great double-sided oak door. 'It's you, Len,' he said, 'what can I do for you?'

'A wire, Master Bowman. Shall I wait for a reply?'

Tom slipped his forefinger into the buff coloured envelope and read the message walking back to Harry in the kitchen. 'CAN YOU DOUBLE YOUR LOADING TO NOTTINGHAM TODAY. JIM CARNOW. What do you think, Harry? We've promised Jim Carnow fifty pots of cabbage.'

'We'll send a hundred,' Harry replied. 'Get the letter book out and send the telegram back. ONE HUNDRED POTS BEING LOADED. BOWMAN AND CARTER.

Tom nipped back to the door and gave young Len from the station the reply. 'That means you and me cabbage cutting today, Harry.'

Harry smiled, saying, 'Seven and six pence a pot.'

Harry and Tom drove down to the cabbage field in the governess cart and were soon bending low over the rows of greens with the sharp hook-bladed knives cutting and throwing the cabbage into heaps. Alf Miller packed each hamper with straw and tied them down with binder twine. Harry, who worked stripped to his waist-coat, took his waistcoat off, throwing it on the hedge, and his knife was so busy he left the other men some yards behind in the rows.

Tom worked close behind him and said, 'Harry, you'll catch your death of cold stripped like that.'

'I'm not made of sugar, Tom. Shan't melt, and I'm thinking one hundred pots of cabbage at seven and six'll buy a good horse.'

Tom, a quiet deep thinking man, found it so invigorating to work with Harry Carter a somewhat tempestous character who had climbed the farming and gardening ladder from the time he worked on the edge of the Cotswolds at Cow Honeybourne. In modern terms Harry was a man whose adrenalin flowed and drove him on and on. He'd listened to Joseph Arch addressing the farm workers of Honeybourne; he cut a field of wheat when only seventeen with hook and crook; harvesting all day without food because his younger brother who was at school forgot to take him his mid-day dinner. Exhausted and feeling so annoyed with his brother, Jim, he went to bed without food and only a cup of water after cutting an acre of wheat.

After the cabbage had been trucked at Ayshon station by Alf and Jack, Harry Carter returned to Stanley Farm to have a meal with Tom Bowman.

'Fancy a bit of home cured, Harry?' Tom asked his partner as he stoked the kitchen grate.

'You know I can, and a couple of eggs. Make the tea strong, Tom. That's to my liking.'

Tom took down a part flitch of fat home-cured bacon off the rack under the white-washed kitchen ceiling. Everything was lime-washed in Tom's kitchen, even the old beams flaked lime off the surface if they were brushed with a broom. The walls were coloured blue, a mixture put on by Sam, the previous tenant of the farm. He made it with lump lime, slaked with size, tallow and washing blue added.

Tom sliced the bacon with his bone-handled carving knife and slung the pan with the hooped handle on the pot hooks over the burning coal. As the two men had their evening meal by the light of an oil lamp swinging on a chain from the beams, enjoying the produce of Tom's yard and Percy Smith's bread from Beckford, Harry looked once more at the *Journal* and exclaimed, 'Let's take the cheque book to Wormington next Wednesday. There's enough money been made out of cabbage this spring to set us up with horses and implements.'

Tom took a teaspoonful of tea from his cup, tasted it, then put in a little more sugar, blew the tea and sipped it, a habit peculiar to Tom. 'Harry,' he said, 'what comes after the cabbage? The beans are blighted, the onions poor.'

Harry scratched his greying hair, looked towards the fire and replied, 'I believe in speculation, as you are aware. Buying in bulk, planting big acreages. If a crop won't sell you lose, but if the price is right you make money.'

'That's as maybe, Harry, but we have got to be careful. Remember that truck of coal you bought cheap delivered to Ayshon station, and we shared it? It's in the coal house now. It won't burn. Twelve tons was a lot to buy on spec. I'll agree to buy some horses and implements if Mr. Bushell will come and advise us.'

'Right,' Harry replied, 'I'll drive you over to the Manor now. First I want a wash and shave. Put another kettle on, Tom, and where's your razor?'

Tom reached up to the shelf above the ingle and gave Harry a black leather case.

'Where did you get this from, it's a bit grand for a village chap?' Harry said as he took the razor from the case.

'Oh, I went with Lily to the Crystal Palace a time back and bought it in London.'

Harry drew Tom's razor backwards and forwards across a sharpening strop which hung from the glass door into the dairy. Then he lathered and shaved at the little wooden-framed looking glass over the sink, and both were ready to visit Fred Bushell. As Tom turned the key in the front door and put it under a slate by the box tree, he smiled saying to Harry, 'Old Durgin always calls that key the blacksmith's daughter. I can't think why.'

At the Manor Fred Bushell was sitting with Ruby in the little room by the walnut tree. This was snug and cosy with the curtains drawn and in daylight he had a view of the yard, the stable and the big barn. 'Come on in, Tom. And, Harry, I hear you have built a fine house in Donnybrook.'

'Yes,' Harry replied, 'but I'm still moving to the Lower Farm at Michaelmas. Tom and I have the tenancy off Arthur Smith.'

'Taking something on,' Ruby joined in the conversation.

'Why?' Harry asked, stroking his moustache.

'You know as well as I do, Harry,' put in Fred Bushell, 'the field by the brook's as full of squitch grass as hell is full of parsons. What are you drinking boys? I know you don't drink cider.'

'Don't worry, Mr. Bushell, Tom and I have just had supper.'

'I've some stone ginger beer in the cellar. Fetch a couple of bottles Ruby.' Ruby came back with the drink and poured some out into two crock cider mugs.

'I suppose you wonder what we have come for this time a night,' Harry said.

'No, no, Harry, you're always welcome here. It's good to have a chat and hear a little of the art and mystery of market gardening.'

Tom told Mr. Bushell how that they had read in the *Journal* about a sale at Wormington.

'Ah, a good farmer is leaving there. Always tops the market with his cattle at Candlemas.'

'It's horses we want and implements, now we are taking over the Lower Farm,' Harry said a bit impatiently, 'and Tom here is a bit nervous of buying.'

Tom, clearing his throat after sipping the stone beer said, 'Would you come and advise us, Mr. Bushell?'

'I'm going there of course, Tom, but once I show an interest in horses the horse copers'll bid more money on purpose to cut me out.'

'I don't want you to bid,' Harry interjected, 'just advise.'

Fred Bushell lit his pipe and sat back in his chair. He winked at

Ruby and Ruby understood as he said, 'Looks like a job for Bert Chandler again.' He explained that when he went horse buying to a farm sale he took Bert Chandler who sat in the stable with his bread and cheese, listening to the talk of the copers as they looked at the horses, and getting into conversation with the carter to find out their good and bad points. 'Bert Chandler and I will meet you at half past ten at the sale and if the horses are as good as I believe them to be, you should get fixed up.'

'We've nothing apart from the gears Min and Tom, our two nags, are harnessed in when we use the drays or the horse hoe,' Tom said.

'Now here's the advantage of buying from a farm sale. You can buy horses' collars, mullins, harness, plough saddles, fillers' gear, long gears, G.O. tackle, all to fit the horses you buy. I'm very particular about harness, especially collars. If they pinch and don't fit snugly you're landed with horses with sore shoulders. Damn bad farming that is.'

Harry smiled and told the fireside friends how that a man was coming back from market down Donnybrook bank and the harness on his horse was all tied up with string. The breeching broke and the poor horse had the back of the shafts against his hocks. Mr. Evans the grocer ran from his shop, looked at the harness and knew that most farmers put on their best tackle to come to town. 'What a set of harness you have got, my man,' the words exploded from Mr. Evans mouth. The carter, not to be outdone, had answered, 'You don't expect us to put on the best of harness just to come to Evesham.' 'The fact was,' Harry explained, 'that that was the only harness the man had got.'

'Ah,' Fred Bushell said,' 'you've never seen Jones and Adam in town looking like rag and bone men. They put on a decent jacket, dubbin their boots, clean the harness and polish the brasses before they take my waggon with a load of corn to the mill in town or take a beast to market in my bull float.'

'Dad's very particular. He's got a notice up in the barn, "A place for everything and everything in its place." '

'Yes, and our place is in bed now, Ruby. Good night, Harry, good night, Tom. I'll see you at Wormington on Wednesday.'

Harry Carter left Donnybrook early on the day of the sale. The iron grey cob showed some white foam under his collar and under the breeching strap.

'You've drove him pretty hard this morning, Harry,' Tom observed as he went to the yard at Stanley Farm to meet his senior partner.

'No, I had my work cut out holding him back. I'll have to go easy on the ground oats I reckon. He's got here in twenty minutes and came like a train up Sedgeberrow Hill.'

The two men sat in the governess cart and were soon away towards the sale. Being early they chose a quiet spot to tie Harry's cob to the rickyard railings. Harry took a little nose bag from under the axle and strapped it on his horse. 'Steady with the oats now, Harry, your cob's pretty prompt you know. Remember when he turned the trap over in Port Street in Donnybrook.'

'Don't worry, Tom. I like my horse to get a move on,' Harry replied.

In the field near the house the farm implements lay on the top of the land. Ploughs, harrows, skims, scuffles, waggons, drays, carts. The harness was all in lots in the barn numbered in sets—such as a set of fillers' gears or shaft harness and so forth. The horses in the stable were tied to the manger, pulling at the clover in the fodder rack above, looking surprised to see so much interest in them this April morning. The carter sat on a wooden corn bin smoking his pipe.

'Morning, carter,' Tom Bowman said as he entered the stable with Harry. 'A sad day for you no doubt.'

'Oi, 'tis in a way, but I'll be satisfied if these dumb animals goes to good homes. I'm gwain to work for Master Hopkins who is taking over the farm, but I think he's got some hosses.'

After a look around the small tools in the cart shed, Harry and Tom met Mr. Bushell and Bert Chandler. Fred Bushell spoke in whispers and taking Tom and Harry aside said, 'Don't be seen in the stable with me, I'm going in alone with the catalogue.'

He went from Lot One, an aged mare named Violet, to the young three-year-old in the loose box, dotting down in his book what he thought each animal was worth.

'Make a note of these figures,' he told the young men, 'but that's providing the horses are sound. There are a couple I wouldn't touch and I've put a cross against them, and the five-year-olds will make a lot of money for town work. Now Bert,' he said to his shepherd, 'here's half a crown, get yourself some bread and ham and a drink of beer at the refreshment bar that Mr. Fletcher from the Hobnails has set up in the end of the cowshed, and don't hang about. Take your food into the stable and just listen to what's said and talk to the carter.'

Bert Chandler sat himself in an empty manger near the Wormington carter. 'Come far, have you?' the carter inquired.

'Under Bredon Hill,' Bert replied.

'Ah, Mr. Bushell farms that part of the country. Do you know him?'

'Ah, a bit,' Bert allowed.

'A good judge of hosses,' the carter said, 'and he's been in here looking um over and I'll warrant he'll buy the best.'

Bert changed the subject, asking the carter how the ground was working and what he thought would happen if the rain didn't come soon.

The carter replied, 'Our gaffer, he's had a fair bit ploughed with the black horses, the steam tackle and the clats be as big as horses' yuds and as hard as the devil's back teeth.'

'Some useful horses here I'd say, but I'm a shepherd and haven't worked with hosses for years, only a nag I ride around the ship.'

'Now Violet, she's as good as gold in the shafts, twelve-year-old mind, but winters well and can be trusted. Somebody ull have a good hoss as buys her. The gelding, the liver chestnut, he's rising seven; pull a house down but you mustn't leave him at the station. Frit to duth a trains.'

Just then a Gloucester horse coper came into the stable with his son, a lad of sixteen. 'Untie that one, my boy,' he called. 'Good worker, ay carter?' he asked.

'They all be good honest workers, as sensible as Christians,' the carter replied. In the stable yard the coper's son led out one animal after another, while his father looked at the horse from behind anxious to see whether their feet were sound and their legs straight.

'I still want a few five- or six-year-olds for a Birmingham brewery,' he told his son, 'and Mr. Cambridge needs a couple more to pull his iron and steel waggon in Smethwick. Whoa,' he called to his boy, and he walked around the back of one useful-looking mare and pulled aside her docked tail. She pottered on the blue brick stable floor. 'Sweet itch that is, son, very difficult to treat.'

'Hers a bit crupper gallded,' the carter said as he left his seat to explain to the dealer.

'Maybe, carter, but why did you let her get like that. Didn't you put some fresh liquour on the crupper? Too much corn they have had and 'tis the humour from high living.'

The coper looked at the next animal and Bert Chandler noted that number six in the catalogue may have sweet itch. As the whole stable of horses was vetted by this coper and local farmers, Bert Chandler pencilled his catalogue. Harry Carter came to the stable, beckoned to Bushell's shepherd saying, 'Mr. Ely is about to sell the horses. Tom and I have bought a couple of waggons, a muck cart, a drill and a Kell plough.'

Tom Bowman handed Bert Chandler's pencilled catalogue to Fred Bushell for his comment. 'Number one seems useful, Tom, that twelve-year-old mare named Violet. We've got to take their word that she is twelve. She's listed as aged. It's a clever man who can tell the age of a horse after it's seven years old.'

'What's the name of the child?' Harry Carter said in a stage whisper to Fred.

'I'll write it against the entry,' Fred said with a laugh, and he passed the catalogue to Harry and Tom. Thirty-five guineas he had written on the paper. 'I like your expression, "What's the name of the child", Harry.'

'Ah, a bit of old Aysum,' Harry replied.

Mr. Ely the auctioneer now called the company to order and opened business. 'Now gentlemen, we start with this aged mare, Violet. There's a good upstanding animal, a good worker in all gears, sound in wind and limb, no vices. A faithful mare with years of work before her, start me at forty guineas.'

'Thirty,' a voice from a man sitting on the fence.

A bad start at thirty. Tom Bowman was to do the bidding.

'Wait a bit, Tom,' Fred said, 'I'll tell you when to bid.'

'At thirty-one guineas. She would suit you, Mr. Bushell.' Fred shook his head and nudged Tom Bowman who bid thirty-two.

'Thirty-two I'm bid, up on the waggon.'

A long pause and the man on the fence put up three fingers.

'Against you, sir, at thirty-three,' Mr. Ely called to Tom. Fred Bushell nudged him again. 'Thirty-four I'm bid. I shan't linger at thirty-four, I'm selling at thirty-four to you, sir,' and Mr. Ely pointed his cane towards the waggon.

'Bowman and Carter, Stanley Farm, Ayshon,' Tom said.

'Ah, yes, Mr. Bushell's tenants.'

The list was gone through and Tom and Harry bought four horses at Wormington from thirty guineas to forty guineas apiece, Violet and Flower, two mares, Captain and Sharper, two geldings. Farming folk tended to be conservative about what they called their farm horses, so there was a small range of names passed on from generation to generation. Harry Carter climbed from the waggon saying, 'Shan't be long, Tom. I'll meet you round the cattle ring.'

Mr. Ely's porter was ringing a bell in the Wormington cow yard and the throng of farmers and dealers were getting their positions to see the first lot of store cattle come into the ring. Harry Carter in the stable found the Wormington carter and waggoner tieing up the horses in their stalls ready for collection by the buyers.

'Can you spare a few minutes, no doubt you could do with a drink?'

'Oi, Master, I be mortal dry. I 'spose 'tis nerves in a manner of speaking, seeing my hosses sold.'

'Come with me to the bar,' and here Harry edged himself to where the trammed barrels were pouring out Flower's best beer. 'A pint of the best and a stone ginger,' he called to the barman.

The carter took the top froth off the ale and left a foaming moustache as he took a deep breath. 'Ah, that's better. Don't you relish a pint on a day such as this, sir?' he asked.

'No, I don't touch it now, but that doesn't mean I don't enjoy seeing someone else drink it.'

'Puts spirit into you, sir, does that,' the carter replied.

'Now come with me to the cart shed and tell me the collars which fit Violet, Flower, Sharper and Captain.'

In the cart shed Harry was told the numbers of the collars for the horses. 'Now Sharper, his shoulders be a bit teart, delicate like, specially on Monday mornings.'

'Collar proud,' Harry replied.

'No, no, he's a good worker but like we, some hosses got tender shins. When you take the collars to the saddlers to have them lined, allus send a fleece of wool down to put anant the straw that ull keep their shoulders in order.' Harry nodded. 'Mullins, sir, they do adjust, but if you want the best I'll pick um out for you.'

'The brasses shine,' Harry remarked.

'Ah now, some waggoners take the brasses and hang um in their cottages. I don't hold with that practice. They belong to the gaffer and now they will belong to you, some on um, if you do buy.'

Harry and Tom bought enough harness for their team. They bought a job lot of bits and pieces to mend, and broken tackle, shut links, buckles, linch pins and a handy box of rivets for mending reins or metre straps.

Harry drove his cob back to the farm house under Bredon Hill. 'Tom,' he said, 'can you take Durgin and Alf over in the morning to bring home the horses and tackle? I'll help Jack to cut a load of cabbage for Nottingham.'

The carter was around the stable at Wormington when Tom arrived with the men next day. He had driven over with Polly, his liver chestnut mare, and the governess cart. The carter helped Durgin to gear the horses and shut them in between the waggon shafts. Captain and Violet were to be fillers in the shafts while Sharper and Flower were put in traces. Then he helped Tom and Durgin lift the Kell plough on to one of the wagons, while Alf put Sharper in front of Violet to pull the other wagon.

'Now back the waggons into the barn when you get home, then have your bait and bring the two fillers up, Violet and Captain, and fetch the muck cart and the corn drill.'

'Right, Master Bowman, as you say,' Durgin replied, and the little caravan which Tom and Harry had bought at Wormington under the edge of the Cotswolds was on its way to a new home under Bredon Hill.

When Durgin passed the Manor cow yard it was gone tea time. Tustin Finch was turning out the milking cows after the half-bred Hereford calves had sucked them dry. He carried a three-gallon bucket half-full of milk for Mr. Bushell's use. 'Got some hosses to look after now, Durgin.'

'Looks like it,' Durgin replied.

'Bist a gwain to feed um on a Sunday or treat like you do your pig and give him enough fittle on Saturday to last the wikend?'

'That's a lie, and you know it. Thee bist a bigger liar than Jack Pepper and he won a belt like that the boxers have for telling lies, so they say.'

'They says as you killed your cockerel because he was treading the hens on a Sunday.'

'That's another abominable lie, but some of us keep the Sabbath and just because you never darken the door of church or chapel, it don't become ya to sneer.' Durgin was quite annoyed at the unreasonable talk of Tustin. He looked in the milk bucket on Tustin's arm and said, 'Nice drop of milk. Who was it milked the wrong cow at Mrs. Smith's a while back? A dry cow, wasn't it?'

Tustin rallied back. 'You have no cause to spread that around. I've been Mr. Bushell's cowman now for three years.'

When Tustin Finch worked for Mrs. Smith at the Grange, old Jarvie Bullock, who had now been dead some years, was cowman. One Sunday Jarvie was taken ill so Mrs. Smith had asked Tustin to see to the cows. Like Fred Bushell's, the cows were used for suckling the calves, but one had to be milked for the house. Tustin was convinced that Peasbrook, a strawberry shorthorn, was the house cow at that time. He struggled for half an hour and managed to extract about half a gallon of doubtful looking liquid. Taking it to the back door of the Grange, he told Mrs. Smith that was all he could get from the house cow. 'That's all right, Tustin, we'll manage. No doubt there will be more in the morning. I expect it's because you are strange to her she won't give her milk down.'

Mrs. Smith had a basin of bread and milk every night before retiring to bed. She put the saucepan on the fire and when it boiled poured the milk into the broken bread and sugar. It looked rather frothy and when she tasted it she said it was salty. Her collie dog refused it. Next morning she said, 'Which cow did you milk last night, Tustin?'

'Peasbrook, m'am,' he replied.

'Bless the boy. She has been dry for two or three months and due shortly to calve.'

Tustin never lived that down and it was ironical that Durgin should know about it. Before he had passed Tom and Harry's house, Tustin called after him, 'It's never fair how cows be treated.'

'Why?' Durgin shouted back.

'They has their tits pulled twice a day and only has a bit of sex once a year.' He laughed and added, 'That's no good for any female.'

'I hope you unt a comparing humans with animals, bwoy,' Durgin replied, ' 'cos man was made in the image of God and Adam was the first in the Garden of Eden.'

'Where did Cain get his Missus from then?'

Durgin ignored this remark from the cowman and joined Alf in the yard of Stanley Farm. 'We are geared up,' Harry Carter told his men in the yard, 'but the farm land is so hard it's impossible to plough. Whenever will it rain?'

Alf Miller put in, 'My Dad was born in 1830 afore the Queen come on the throne, and he says he's never known a spring like it. Why, the ground's as hard as the devil's back teeth.'

It was on a Saturday dinner time in April that Jim Cambridge arrived at Ayshon railway station on the two twenty train from Birmingham to visit his farm. The sun was quite hot as he walked over the level crossing to the opposite platform and booking office; such a day that Bert Chandler described as a weather breeder, 'Too summer-like for April.'

Jim pushed the first class ticket into Len the porter's hand, together with a shilling. 'I see my wire has been delivered which I sent from the office this morning, and Ralph's here with the trap.'

Len touched his hat, straightened his sleeved waistcoat and replied, 'Yes, sir, I delivered it at eleven o'clock.'

The plum blossom in the Groaten field hung on the trees snow white against the green backcloth of Bredon Hill. The cottagers' bees were doing their work busily pollinating the blow. As the two men drove through the Groaten Lane together to Jim's weekend cottage the iron master looked across the Wynch field to the house he hoped to buy later in the year. 'I feel I should be spending more time here under Bredon away from the smoke and dust of the iron works.' Ralph nodded and gave a grunt. 'You don't know how people live up in Birmingham and the Black Country, Ralph. The scent of the blossoms here and the peace, it woos me.'

'Do it, Gaffer? The wheat under the 'lectric looks kind.'

'I'll see that later, when I've looked at my daffodils in the orchard.'

'You won first prize with the blooms at Stanway show, your King Alfreds do take some licking, sir.'

'Yes, Ralph, yes, but here's Mr. Bushell. Pull the horse up by the Cross, I'd like a word with him.'

'Ah, James, nice to see you, and what a champion day,' Fred Bushell greeted his friend from the Midlands.

'Can you come along to the cottage tonight, Fred? I've a case or so of rather good wine I bought from a friend in the trade in Birmingham. And Ralph has bottled some of the cider we made at your place last November.'

'I'd be pleased to, Jim. How's the wheat doing under the electric?'

'Ralph says it's looking rather well.'

As Jim's man put the horse and trap away, Jim sauntered among his daffs, looking at the blossoms above in his orchard. Every tree had a name printed with a label on its trunk. He chanted them over to himself. The plums were Rivers Early Prolific, Belle de Louvoir, Victoria, Jimmy More, Warwickshire Droopen, the Clapp, Favourite Pears, William Bon Creitun, Burgandy Windsor, Pitmaston Duchess.

The apple trees were not in full bloom. The pink buds were just bursting among the pale green leaves. Jim halted under a Worcester Pearmain. He looked at its trunk and noticed that for about twelve inches from the grass the trunk was peeled of its bark. The next one had a similar peeling of the bark. Jim ran to the garden where Ralph was working with plants on a hot bed of stable manure under a glass frame and shouted, 'Ralph, I'm ruined, I'm ruined.'

'Why, Gaffer, what ever's up?'

'Something has barked my Worcester Pearmain trees. They'll die!'

Ralph followed his master to the orchard and saw that the rabbits off the hill had barked several trees. 'What can be done, man?' Jim called almost in tears.

'I'll fix um,' Ralph replied, 'but we better put wire guards on the rest.' Ralph took a bucket to the stable and shovelled some horse manure into it, then dug some clay from the garden and mixed it up like a cement and plastered the trees where the rabbits had eaten the bark. 'There sir, that'll prevent them drying out,' and he wrapped up the injured trees in some sacking bandages.

Ralph went home at four-thirty, it being Saturday, leaving Jim Cambridge alone with his thoughts. He went to the vegetable garden, looked at the freshly dug patch all ready for the summer cabbage plants. He walked to the cold frame and pulled one hundred plants from the plant bed. Returning to the patch he took a spade and began laboriously setting the cabbage in a row, digging holes one foot apart.

Old Bert Chandler looked over the hedge from Church Close where he had been feeding the ewes and lambs. 'Gaffer,' he began, 'you wants a setting pin for that caper.'

'A setting pin?' Jim replied.

'Ah, a dibber to plant the cabbage, you understand my meaning. 'Tis a tool, sir, made from a broken fork stale, the crutch end sharpened to a point. I'll fetch mine from the cottage. You be more than welcome to borrow him.' Bert came back with his dibber and showed Jim how to set the plants.

At seven o'clock Fred Bushell arrived and he and Jim sat under the blossoming trees on a garden seat sampling Jim's wine. 'A sad job with my Worcester Pearmains, Fred. The rabbits have barked them.'

'You need some cow muck or horse muck and clay to stop them drying out,' Fred replied.

'Ralph's already done that, but I'm worried about losing the trees.'

'Now look here, Jim, what Ralph does, that will be the right thing. They say in Ayshon that Ralph's got green fingers.'

'I suppose so,' Jim replied. 'Come and look at my strawberries just coming into bloom.'

The two men stood for a while at the end of the strawberry rows. Fred said, 'What do you feed them on?'

'Oh, Ralph's got some idea that liquid feed from that hogshead barrel is a tonic to the plants. It's made from the soiled wool Bert Chandler clips from your sheep, mixed with soot and rain water.'

Fred looked into the barrel replying, 'Belting from the ewes. Now that's what Bert clips from their tail end before the June shearing. It does make a good liquid fertiliser. What's Ralph done to the hawthorn tree, Jim? I see he's cut the branches off it.'

'Grafted it with Pitmaston Duchess pears. He says it's an idea he had from his grandfather,' Jim explained.

The grafts fixed with clay on the hawthorn boughs stuck up on the tree top like a hat stand. Fred smiled, 'Between the two of you, Jim, you're doing a mixture between the best of the old ways and the new, with Ralph's grandfather's grafting and your electrifying wheat fields. What are you planting in the Bank Piece this year? I see it's ploughed but still not planted.'

'Potatoes,' Jim replied. 'We shall plant in July to get young potatoes for Christmas. I know the yield 'll be light, but there 'll be a demand from the Birmingham hotels for young potatoes at that time of the year. You know, Fred, I'm convinced that if produce can be marketed out of season, that's what pays. Take my hens for instance, they lay all winter.'

Jim's fowl house had half a dozen acetylene lamps which were alight all night in the winter, and, as Jim said, 'The hens think it's spring all the year round. Some lay two eggs in twenty-four hours.'

During the dry spring of 1911, Jim Cambridge diverted a stream off Bredon Hill to his early potato field next to the Bank Piece where the 'lates' were to grow. He'd planted Sharpes Express in November and by April the rows were green as the cunningly arranged irrigation trenches flowed with spring water and flooded the hungry tubers. Watercress grew below the sheep wash pool.

In Jim's greenhouse great leaves of tobacco dried and cured under the roof. He grew a quarter of an acre on some damp black soil near Paris. 'But, Jim, you smoke Havana cigars. Why grow tobacco?' Fred enquired.

'My men at the foundry smoke their clay pipes and a number of them chew the weed at work. The tobacco doled out on pay day keeps them in good heart at their work. And another thing, Fred, last summer I went to Jersey and saw the huge cabbages growing for cattle feed and the stems being used for walking sticks. I brought back an ounce or so for seed, planted it in the greenhouse and am hoping to grow a crop and maybe go into the walking stick trade if we have a good summer, which seems likely. I'll get the stems worked in Birmingham. It's great fun doing something different.'

'All very interesting, Jim, to a man like me who aims at selling one thousands pounds-worth of fat cattle from the Dean every autumn.'

'When I come to Ayshon I hope to grow mushrooms in the cellar of the Wynch Farm. Already my pastures have been planted with spawn and dressed with salt and soot.'

Fred replied, 'Now, Jim, if you want mushrooms, fill your fields with horses. They'll follow horses, but stallions are best, I don't know why. I suppose you know Harry Carter and Tom Bowman are growing sprouts on my hill land, they ought to come and see you. Harry Carter's a shrewd market gardener from Evesham.'

As the light failed the two men went into the house. Jim's maid, Mabel, brought in the cheese board and the crusty bread from Harry Court's bakehouse and they sampled the bottled cider. At ten o'clock Fred left for the Manor, leaving Jim with his thoughts and ideas of scientific farming.

The clay land of the Evesham Vale grew heavy crops of almost anything if the soil could be, as Bert Chandler said, 'harnessed'. After the winter rains and the March winds the weather had a cementing effect on the clay if no late frosts came to freeze the furrows, breaking the soil (called heavy) but in fact light, into a crumb-like mould.

That April the Thurness field was much too hard and dry for a team of horses to plough. At best the share would only sink six or seven inches when the season was right. Tom Bowman had seen Squire Baldwyn's iron horses, as he called them, breaking up the fallow ground under Bredon.

In the first place, the Squire used one engine positioned on the headland with an anchor on the opposite side. The cable from the revolving drum under the engine extended to the anchor. Ploughing was done in a clockwise fashion around the field, but soon the Squire purchased two engines; the cable ran fast and loose between them on the opposite headlands. Fireman Davies drove one of these engines. The Squire's carter rode on the plough or cultivator.

Harry Carter as a boy had worked on land where Bomford's cultivating engines were fairly common on some of the large fields around Honeybourne. It was much easier to work the larger fields—when the equipment was set up the men could do a respectable acreage per day. Three men were needed to work the tackle; an engine driver on each engine and one man riding the plough.

Another man would be employed with a cart drawing the water for the boilers and coal to make the steam.

So in 1911 when horse ploughing was out of the question owing to the state of the ground, Harry Carter biked to Didcot where the Winchcombe Thrashing and Steam Cultivating Company, a contracting firm run by Mr. Edwards, had their engines ploughing the stubble for the farmer at Didcot Farm. On his way back from Didcot he saw the little gardeners of Grafton planting sprout plants with crow bars and watering them with buckets and tin cans. The sun and the drying wind faded the tiny plants before the men got to the end of each row. There's faith for you, he thought.

Stodge, who rode the steam plough, and the two drivers arrived at Thurness with the caravan in which they lived and set up their tackle on that twenty-two acres of clay. One engine in the outfit had pulled the plough and cultivator, while the other had pulled the caravan with the water cart behind. Stodge had surveyed the job and was oiling the wheels of the cultivator when Harry and Tom arrived. He turned to greet them with, 'Don't the wheels ever hoot for want of oil! They was enough to charm a fella coming from Didcot.'

'Which do you advise, the plough or cultivator, Stodge?' Harry Carter questioned.

'Oi, the scuffle,' indicating the cultivator with an oily rag. 'Let the sun on the clats and it will be as good as a dressing of muck. Why, the mon as worked the land afore you chaps never ploughed above four inches deep. You'll fallow it this year, I spose?'

Harry turned to Tom. 'What do you think, Tom?'

Tom replied, 'Yes, we'll fallow most of it. We may plant a little if we can ever get it down to a tilth.'

Little Durgin arrived with his frail basket of food and his tea. He threw his jacket down under the roadside hedge and his dog, Tiny, lay on it beside the frail. Durgin had Violet between the shafts of a muck cart loaded with coal. He unhooked his horse leaving the loaded cart on the headland for the drivers to stoke up from. He put Violet in the shafts of the water cart and went to the spring of water beside the turnpike road. The spring, despite the drought, was running well, the watercress green on its bank and the minnows, coloured like miniature mackerel, swimming in the clear water. The steam waggons with loads of Canadian wheat from Avonmouth

Docks were continually calling for water from that spring en route to Birmingham. Durgin dropped the hose pipe in the spring and pushed and pulled the water pump handle, counting the strokes until he knew that the water tank was full before he drew his load to the engines on the headland.

Young Adam was also in the field. He shut off at three o'clock for his usual late dinner, which he ate on the Thurness headland. As the engine took on water from Durgin's cart, Stodge turned to Adam. 'Would you like to ride this yer thing for a bout? My ass is sore and it's a rough road to Dublin.'

Adam looked at the driver who nodded consent. He then mounted the iron seat of the scuffle and held the heavy steering wheel in his hands. 'Mind and keep a straight mark, my boy. The tother engine ull pull ya straightish to the headland, but you must steer that front wheel and keep the tool from wandering.'

On a small sack of hay Adam sat as Stodge described him, 'like a tom tit on a leg of mutton', bouncing over the rough hard ground. As the engine opposite puffed the smoke, tightened the cable, Adam was riding a mechanical cultivator in his first year of farm work.

Tom told the men to water the sprout plants in Stanley Farm garden ready to pull and set on Bredon Hill. 'Take a hogshead barrel on the muck cart, Durgin, and fill it at the moat pond.'

Alf, Jack and Durgin pulled twenty-five thousand plants and put them in the shade in the big barn. Tomorrow they were to make history planting sprouts on Bredon. Harry and Tom walked up the hill that evening and found the ridges of soil still damp over the limestone rock. As Harry picked up one flat stone after another, he said, ' 'Tis the stones that hold the moisture.'

When Durgin took the hampers of plants up the hill the next morning with the dray, he had Violet in the shafts and Sharper in traces in front. Alf, Jack, Tom and Harry joined him at the hamlet of Paris and walked by the side of the dray. Harry took the first handful of plants from a hamper and with his setting pin lead the team of five men across the field setting his plants a yard apart. The work went like wildfire, good planting, except when the pin hit a hidden stone and jarred their wrists.

'Set them firm and deep on the moisture,' Harry told the men, 'and

I reckon they will grow.' Tom impressed them to handle the roots carefully and retain the mop of fibre which they had grown in the garden. By half past five the twenty-five thousand plants were set and the men with aching backs rode down the hill on the dray with Durgin holding the reins on Violet. Sharper, in front, kept to the track made by horses for generations and the dray wheels followed the ruts made by immemorial carts and waggons.

So five acres of the fifteen acre field were planted the first day. The plants grew on the hill and Harry's parsley came up on the headland while the crops on the clay in the Vale were baked in the sun.

From the barn the smoke and steam of the cultivating engines in Thurness could easily be seen. The driver decided that the heavy scuffle would be better to penetrate the rock-like clay and told Bowman and Carter that with their consent he would use that heavy cultivator. As Stodge, the little man who rode the implement, bounced over the ground and the scuffle reared, pitched and tossed, the steel feet on the legs of this massive implement were broken under the strain. When the field was ploughed thirty years after, the plough brought these broken feet up to the surface. But as Stodge had said, the heavy clay clats when laved by the sun and the rain which would eventually come, made fertile loam for a crop of corn.

So the two extremes of Bowman and Carter's farming went forward. A struggle for existence by the sprout plants and they survived, and a struggle by Stodge and the engine drivers to break up the fallow ground of Thurness.

5

Oak Apple Day

MAY DAY IS LOOKED FORWARD TO BY THE FARMING community as the day when the yarded cattle are turned out into the fields. But Fred Bushell, like some of the dyed in the wool traditionalists of the hill villages, recognised Old May Day from the old calendar as the day for the great exodus from the cattle yards. As Harry Carter planted his runner beans on the 12th May or Stow Fair Day, so Fred Bushell observed Old May Day.

> When the elm leaf is as big as a farthing
> It's time to plant runner beans in the garden.
> When the elm leaf is as big as a penny
> You will have to plant if you are going to have any.

Harry knew that by planting his beans as late as 12th May he would miss the spring frosts. Fred knew that by keeping his cattle yarded until 11th they wouldn't meet the growing grass but the fields of grass keep would be grown away in front of his animals.

May 1911 was a little different. The continued drought had stunted the growth of everything. As Fred turned his half-bred Hereford yearling bullocks into the Manor pastures he noted that the grass wasn't tall enough to hide a hare. 'How many loads of mangolds are still in the bury, Tustin?' he asked his cowman.

'Oh, there could be twenty cartloads, Master,' Tustin replied.

'Make a load last three days and draw the cart alongside the hedge in the Dean,' were Fred Bushell's instructions. 'Throw the mangolds over the hedge and draw each cartload into a different place and feed the bullocks every morning as soon as you have suckled the calves,' he added.

From the newly formed West Midland Farmers Association the

farmer of the Manor ordered a truck of cotton and linseed cattle cake. Bert Chandler sawed feeding tubs for the bullocks out of half nine-gallon barrels. Each animal was given several pounds of cake each day to supplement the scarcity of the grass. In Cinder Meadow where the fattening bullocks had been moved after outwintering on Bredon Hill, Tustin Green and Ruby fed more cake to fatten the bullocks.

On Fred Bushell's fifteen acre field by Great Hill Barn, Durgin Green worked alone hoeing the charlock from the rows of sprout plants. The nine hundred foot high Bredon Hill land was still moist under the limestones which lay among the crop like small frying pans.

Durgin just whispered, 'Blast,' to himself every time his hoe plate struck a stone, sending an electric-like shock up his arms, bare to the sun. He never used language any stronger than blast, being devout Chapel. He sang as he hoed an old hymn, 'Dare to be a Daniel. Dare to stand alone.' Tustin, always teasing the little man, said that Durgin once got very excited as he testified at an open air chapel meeting. 'How would you feel if one morning you woke and found yourself dead?' he said to the villagers. 'In the bottom of the bottomless pit of Hell. Where should you be then?' Durgin took all these insults in good part, telling Tustin that he prayed for him every night that he might see the light.

After Fred Bushell's calves had had their evening milk, Tustin walked across the knap by the Cuckoo Pen on purpose to meet Durgin as he carried his empty frail dinner basket back home through the Paris Gardens.

'My runner beans be in flower,' he said to Bowman and Carter's man.

'Don't tell such abominable lies, it don't become ya,' Durgin replied. 'Runner beans beant planted until Stow Fair on 12th May.'

From his jacket Tustin took a tobacco tin and showed Durgin six runner bean seeds in wheat flour. 'Now say they are not in flower,' he said.

Durgin laughed at the remark which he called foolhardy and told Tustin, 'Master Bushell ought to give thee an extra bob a wick for being in the know.'

Down in the Thurness field Harry Carter, Tom Bowman, Alf Miller and Jack Gardener were chiselling away at the weeds with

their hoes among the early Telegraph peas. A lot of the land lay
fallow behind the steam ploughs, but Harry had planted a sack of
peas on a bit of lighter land near the turnpike road in February. Tom
and Harry's bikes were propped up against the signpost near the
gate.

'Looks like a milestone inspector coming from Asyum,' Alf said
to Harry Carter. They bent their backs and continued the hard
slogging, hoeing among the peas. 'It's a black man, you chaps,' Jack
Gardener exclaimed, 'and he's catching hold of a bike!'

In a flash the man off the road mounted a bike and pedalled
furiously towards Tewkesbury. 'It's Tom's bike!' Harry said as he
was the first to run to the gateway.

Tom Bowman decided to stop the first car which came from
Evesham way and the other men went on to work. 'A fella has just
stolen my bike,' he called through the side screen of the two seater
and dickey car, 'can you give me a lift?'

'Jump in, I'm going to Cheltenham,' the driver replied. Tom sat in
front carrying his twelve bore gun and placed it between his knees.
'A farmer, no doubt young man,' the driver ventured.

'Well, just starting, my partner and I rent land off the gentleman at
the Manor,' Tom replied. At Pinch Loaf cottages—so named because
a baker of years ago gave short weight with his loaves of bread,
pinching the loaf—the driver and Tom spotted the black man pedal-
ling for all he was worth towards Beckford Inn. 'Drop me off fifty
yards ahead of him, please, then I can stop him,' Tom asked the car
driver.

As the cyclist approached Tom Bowman, Tom went through the
motions of putting a couple of Crimson Flash cartridges in the
breech of his gun and pointing it towards the black man. As the man
fell from the bike, he threw his arms in the air in surrender saying,
'Don't shoot me, Master! Think of my poor mother in Cardiff. She
wants to see her boy.'

'I shan't shoot you, but you will come with me to Sergeant
O'Rourke at Beckford and he has a place to lock you up before you
go to Gloucester Jail.'

'My poor old mother in Cardiff!' the man wailed.

'Ah, but you should have thought of her when you stole my bike,'
Tom said.

'I'll work for you, Master, if you don't take me to the police,' was the reply.

The two men reached Beckford Inn, the black man still pleading with Tom whose heart softened when he thought of some poor woman in Cardiff waiting for her son. Tom took a label from his jacket pocket with the legend printed on it, 'Bowman and Carter, Farmers and Market Gardeners. Stanley Farm, Ayshon, Glos.' 'Here,' he said, putting the label in the man's hand, 'this is our address. I'll give you half an hour to be at my house or else I'll put the police on you.'

Tom mounted his bike, rode past the Grafton crossroads, saluted Fred Bushell and Ruby as they were penning their ewes ready for shearing, and waited at the farm house door. Thirty minutes later the black man arrived at Stanley Farm.

'My eyes, he's in a hurry, no ordinary milestone inspector, I reckon,' Tustin said to Adam as he passed the Grafton fingerpost.

Out of breath he met Tom Bowman at the yard gate. Tom took his watch from his pocket and said, 'I was giving you another five minutes afore I fetched the policeman from his cottage.'

'Master, Master, what work do you want done? I do anything,' the man replied.

'Can you drink a cup of tea and eat some bread and cheese?' Tom replied. 'And just climb the ladder to the tallet over the stable and make yourself a bed among the hay.'

'Yes Master. Thank you. I'll eat the bread and cheese and I'm thirsty. Some tea please,' was the reply.

'One week you will work for us and that's where you will sleep,' Tom continued, pointing to the door at the top of some steps over the stable, an old bothy, where the single men lived when they ploughed the Stanley Farm fields years ago.

'Can't send him hooving,' Harry Carter said that evening in Tom's kitchen. Harry was particular who hoed, or hooved, his crops and didn't want his Telegraph peas spoilt.

'I bin thinking, Harry, the cattle yard was left full of muck by Fred Bushell's last tenant. It needs cleaning and the muck carted to the field we'll be planting mangolds in next year. Durgin and this chap could have a week shifting that.'

Next morning Durgin hooked Captain in a muck cart and he and the black man were soon busy forking the yard muck into the cart and taking the loads to the mangold field. 'What be I to call tha, ay?' Durgin said to his new mate.

'Call me Sam, for that's my name, sir,' he replied.

'They call me Durgin, but don't call me sir. I'll be talked about else,' the little man replied.

Durgin and Sam got on so well together that on the Sunday they both went to chapel. One thing that Durgin couldn't understand; every morning when Tom fried the fat home-cured bacon Durgin took some to the bothy, but it was always uneaten. 'Sam ant yut his fettle agun, good bacon and all, drinks his tea and puts a bit of fat on his bread, but leaves the bacon. Perhaps they don't yut such fittle where he comes from.'

At the end of the week Tom gave Sam a sovereign to help him on his way and Annie Green gave him a pair of her knitted socks. I like to think that some poor widow woman in Cardiff welcomed her boy, his character still unblemished, although he took Tom's bike.

Towards the end of May Ruby Bushell and old Bert Chandler sheared the sheep from the Manor in the thatched barn near the village cross. From dawn until dusk they worked their hand shears and turned out the ewes into the orchard where the bleating of sheep and the call of their lambs made rustic music for half the village to hear.

Durgin Green lived what he called, 'Anant the barn by the walnut tree. They charms me and the Missus every morning soon after four o'clock, but they be glad to loose their jackets no doubt this muggy weather.' It was so true that the unsheared part of Fred's flock spent their day panting under the orchard boughs and not until night time did they graze the scanty sward of the orchard.

'Restless the cows be, Master, when I suckles the calves these afternoons,' Tustin remarked to Fred Bushell. ' 'Tis comical to see them with their tails up in the air galloping away from the torment of the bree flies under Mrs. Price's Jargonelle pear tree, then under the drooping ash on their road to the Brook Meadows,' he said with a half-witted laugh.

Tustin, although he was so stupid in his remarks, especially to old Durgin, was a good stockman. 'Stockmen are born not made,' Fred Bushell said to Tom Bowman. 'Brought up by his father, in a way tied to a cow's tail.' Tom just nodded, listening to his landlord. 'It's not the smart young chaps with collars and ties and fancy waistcoats that suit me for my work,' Fred added. 'Take Adam Hunt, he had never handled a fleece of wool until this shearing, now one or two lessons from Bert Chandler and he rolls as good a fleece from the shearers as I have seen. You could play football with them, they'd never come undone.'

As they spoke in the yard at the Manor, Mrs. Price arrived all agitated. 'Mr. Bushell,' she began, 'your cows have rubbed against my pear tree and knocked all the fruit off and Tustin just laughs. I'll make you pay for that, sir,' she said in a voice of vinegar.

Fred was quite unmoved, but Tom could see from past experience that his mind was working very fast indeed. As she left the yard Fred turned to Tom and said, 'People who live in glass houses shouldn't throw stones.' Tom was not sure what Fred was thinking until Fred said in a whisper, 'I carry a stone in my pocket a long while before I throw it, but I shall throw it.'

'I see,' Tom replied.

'Ah, you know I've been good to Mrs. Price letting her fowls scratch for corn after the thrashing. In fact they are always in my rick yard. She will be told to keep them at home now. How's Harry by the way?'

Tom Bowman related the story of how he and Harry were pigeon shooting on the hill when Harry was suddenly taken by a severe attack of lumbago. 'I had to leave him by the barn and fetch Min and the dray to take him down to the village. Then I drove him to Evesham with Polly and my governess cart. I stayed in Evesham that night, Alice Carter put me up. He's a lot better though, since going for treatment.'

'Some quack they say,' Fred replied.

'Sequar, the Red Indian bone setter, treated him. I took him by train to Gloucester. Harry walked on two sticks and when we got into Sequar's rooms in Barton Street the bone setter's appearance was frightening, but Harry was in such pain he would face almost anything.'

The tall red-skinned man had worn a head-dress of feathers and a suit of animal skins. Around the room were testimonials from great men of all nationalities who had been successfully treated by him. Harry lay helpless on the table. At first Sequar gently massaged his back with some strong smelling oils, a secret substance shared by no one. Then he worked harder until beads of perspiration fell from his nose. He manipulated Harry's legs, stretched his arms, then after three quarters of an hour's treatment told him to dress, charging him two pounds for the treatment and five shillings for a bottle of embrocation.

Harry had walked back to Gloucester Station carrying his walking sticks under this arm. Harry was better and on the Saturday night Alf Miller's wife went into Evesham with her new babies to see him. 'Didn't welcome her,' Alice Carter remarked to Tom. 'Coming here before she had been churched, there will like enough be a baby in this house now within twelve months.'

But Durgin Green was pleased to see his master about again.

'Didn't like to tell ya bout the time I went to Sequar in Aysum market place,' Durgin said. 'One Saturday night I was amus mad a the tuth ache. My old yud he did ache and the one eye tuth a mine jumped like a jumping jack.'

Durgin sucked his breath between his toothless gums and continued, 'On this Saturday night Sequar was tooth drawing opposite the Public Hall. He exed anybody that was suffering to step in the chair. I sat down in the chair in the middle of a great ring of folk and waited for him to come with his pincers. A brass band was playing but twas not a patch on Salvation Army.

' "Which tooth, young fella?" he said above the din. I said, "All on um, Gaffer," and that was a mistake. Sequar grabbed the first tooth, threw it to the crowd and the band played louder. The drummer did tabber his drum and struck the cymbals. I tried to hit Sequar but his tough horny hand held me down.

'I kicked his shins, but he said, "You want um all out young fella." He gave me a cup of water and I spet blood all up Bridge Street, and mother never recognised me when I got home. My face was swelled like a bucket, my eyes were bunged up as if I bin to a wasp's nest. Next morning I couldn't eat. I lived on cocoa sop for a fortnight. Mind you, his cough lozenges did Alf Miller's Ida good though, so she says, and the physic was very strong.' Alf Miller came up at that moment and heard what they were saying. 'Ay,' he agreed, 'I remember this prattle that foggy night in Asyum. He had slept in a damp bed in Broddy and spoke with a husky voice. "Take one lozenge and place it on the top of the tongue and let it dissolve," he says. Then his voice becomes clearer and he finishes up roaring like a bull. "You can't get it from Boots's! You can't get it from Elliots's! You can't get it from Craven's! Only Sequar who brings to you the secrets of the Red Man." '

'By the way, Master Carter,' Durgin put in, changing the subject, 'the Cricket Committee meets on Monday to pick the team for Saturday against Norton and Lenchwick. Now we would like to see you at the match 'cos I reckon they ull pick Master Bowman in the team.'

'I'll see,' Harry replied, 'but it's usual for me to spend Saturday afternoon in Evesham.'

'Michaelmas you take over the Lower Farm ent it? I look forrard to having you living there with just an orchard between your house and my thatched cot at the Cross,' Durgin replied.

Durgin who suffered so much leg-pulling from Tustin and sneers from Singer Sallis found in Harry and Tom two men who were of the same persuasion as himself, noncomformists and abstainers. The partners however were blessed with more intelligence than their worker Durgin. They had the happy knack of being tolerant to the cider and beer drinking, gambling villagers without departing from their strong principles. Harry had been generous to the newly formed Cricket Club which did not go unnoticed by the Reverend Rushton or Singer Sallis at the White Hart.

The Cricket Committee met on that Monday in the middle of May 1911 in what was known as the pavilion, an old Midland Railway carriage which stood under the hedge near the main road on Frank Bishop's Broadenham field. Reverend Rushton and Frank Bishop, both dyed in the wool Tories, had been upset when the side of the carriage had been pastered with Liberal slogans by some of the farm workers of Ayshon. It was generally believed that young Ruby Bushell had been at the back of this; Ruby did those sort of things more for devilment than to support the Radicals.

In the Minute Book the record says:

Committee Meeting May 13th, 1911 after practice (held in the pavilion.

It was proposed by Rev. Rushton and seconded by Mr. F. Bishop that Mr. Bushell junior be struck off the Committee and George

Weston be elected in his place. The team was picked to play Norton and Lenchwick.

It included Tom Bowman and young Adam Hunt. Bert Chandler was chosen as umpire for the season. Bert Chandler said to Tom Bowman as they walked up Gypsy's Lane after practice, 'If you be to get on at cricket or at church in this parish it pays to hold the candle to the parson and to Frank Bishop. Ruby's a silly young devil. He unt worth his father's shoe strings, no, not a hatful of crabs. Moderation in all things, Tom, you'll agree.'

Tom Bowman just nodded then said, 'When the drink gets the better of a chap it's the time to sign the pledge. I got the young blacksmith to sign when he was seventeen. He could see what the drink did for his father.'

'Ah, old George used to be drunk at half past six in the morning in the smithy in Blacksmith's Lane, but I bin moderate and never abused myself and a pint of beer won't keep me or anyone else out of Heaven when my times comes. Don't you ever fancy a pint, Tom?' Fred Bushell's old shepherd questioned.

Tom Bowman then told the shepherd how one night at Evesham Mop he was the worse for drink and he challenged anyone to fight him outside the Red Horse pub, a foolish thing for a lad of seventeen to do.

'You and Harry are both in the Salvation Army now, unt ya?'

'Yes, and it's one of the old General's articles of war, but I don't expect men of the land like you to abstain altogether.'

Bert Chandler then said that when he was weaned from what they called the titty bottle, he went straight on to cider, the only thing that would stop him crying for the milk. ' 'Tis a funny old world, Tom,' he said.

Adam was curious to see how the publican from the White Hart prepared the field for the game. He had seen the cricket fields of Overbury and the billiard table wicket of Dumbleton, but now he'd been sent by Fred Bushell to help Singer Sallis early on the morning of the first match in the Broadenham field. Adam had arrived with Noble and one of Fred Bushell's drays with a hogshead cider barrel full of water. 'Now draw your dray alongside where I've mowed the wicket, bwoy,' Singer instructed.

Adam did as he was told and he and Singer tapped the barrel then proceeded to fill their watering cans fitted with roses to water the twenty-two yards of parched brown turf between the wickets. When the barrel was empty Singer said, 'Now we will have our bait. I brought you a bottle of Rowland's beer to have with your thumb piece of bread and cheese.'

Under the elms by the turnpike road man and boy sat in the shade. 'There's a little iron shuppick in my cart in Gypsy's Lane, and a wheelbarrow. Just fetch it, will ya.' Adam did as he was told and Singer walked towards the stile where the footpath leads to Bury's orchard, pulled the iron roller from under the hedge to the wicket and started to roll the pitch. 'Here, Adam, bring me the barrow and the fork. Wheel the barrow to the boundary and I'll show you what to do.'

The outfield of Broadenham had been grazed by Frank Bishop's cattle. A couple of strands of barbed wire had kept the animals off the wicket, but cow pats, pancakes, as they were called, were scattered all over the field. 'Now, Adam, these dollups of muck from Frank's cattle are dried hard in the sun, but we don't want the fielders to be hampered by such things. Pick them up on the shuppick fork and wheel them to the hedge and make a clear sweep. Start like you would with a mowing machine and circuit the field, then you will finish by me at the wicket in the middle.'

By twelve o'clock Singer had rolled and re-rolled the pitch until a favourable wicket was formed and Adam had cleared the cow pats from the outfield.

'Put the barrow and fork back into my cart and bring me a straight edge of wood and a whitewash brush,' commanded the inn keeper. Singer Sallis then drew the creases at each end of the wicket. Next he unlocked the railway carriage pavilion, taking from the rack a well worn cricket bat and ball. Singer hammered in the stumps without the bails. 'Here, bwoy,' he said. 'Take this bat and I'll toss a few balls to ya.'

Adam squared up to the bowler, blocking the balls in a nervous manner as they pitched on the watered turf. 'What's the wicket like, Mr. Sallis?' Adam asked the bowler after he'd sent six balls down towards the stumps.

'Ay, the ball comes through nice and even, but no doubt Arthur

Jackson 'll get some pace out of it,' Singer answered. They then went home to their mid-day dinner and got ready for the match.

Ayshon cricketers were an odd assortment as regards their dress that Saturday afternoon. Some had grey flannels and wore their pancake-type caps as they wore on Sundays. Arthur Jackson was all in his white attire with the regulation studded boots—he'd played many times for other villages. Tustin had white flannels and a striped shirt, but his trousers were held in place by braces. Ruby Bushell, who had been to the Grammar School, wore his old blazer over the white shirt and trousers. He sported a blue cap with a pale blue ribbon surround—an old one from school.

On this first match it was only expected that the players' appearance would not be uniform. The village had struggled to get the gear and the pavilion. Fred Bushell promised to help any players who could not afford the regulation white outfit. Young Adam had been measured by Harry Bittridge at the Bon Marche for trousers and blazer. The colour chosen by the committee was navy blue with canary yellow, later to be known as 'Ayshon Tigers.'

Harry Carter arrived at the Broadenham field with the iron grey cob, Dick, pulling his governess cart at a cracking pace. 'Yer comes Master Carter,' Tustin said, as he and young Adam lay with their ears on the turnpike road listening to the sound of Dick's hooves beating on the blue hill stone. Harry sat by his landlord, Fred Bushell, in the shade of the crab apple tree just off the field boundary.

A handsome pair they looked. Fred Bushell dressed in tweed breeches, cloth gaiters, a Norfolk jacket, and Harry, as usual, in fawn drill trousers, no jacket or waistcoat, a new panama hat, and wearing what he called his tea drinkers, his light weight boots.

Norton and Lenchwick batted first and faced the bowling of Jones and Singer Sallis. The runs came steadily then. Reverend Rushton put himself on to bowl with young Adam Hunt. Adam soon had a wicket and then another, but the Norton men punished the parson's bowling. Fred Bushell signalled to Reverend Rushton as they changed over and as he came towards the boundary Fred called, 'Try Arthur Jackson.'

Arthur, that dog and stick farmer from the Wood Farm, took a long run to the wicket, but had three wickets in his first over. 'Useful bowler,' Harry Carter remarked to Fred Bushell.

'Yes, Harry, Arthur once bowled out W. G. Grace at a charity match when he played for Overbury. The umpire shouted, "No ball!" just as the great man's middle stump went pitchpolling down the field. "But I bowled him," Arthur replied. The umpire—he was an old gardener from the Court—said, "Folks be come yer to see Grace bat, not to see thee bowl." '

Norton made sixty-seven runs all out that May day on the Broadenham and at tea time down came the rain. A pity, the result had to be a draw. As the two teams sat in the railway coach pavilion and watched the storm lash the wicket, the farming folk hoped that the drought would be over, but the thunder moved over Bredon Hill and the parched earth soaked the rain like blotting paper.

'Now Singer, perhaps you could entertain our guests,' the parson said. Singer took a large red and white spotted handkerchief from his jacket pocket and told Tustin to put his arm in a sling. He sent Adam over the road to coalman Haines' cottage where Gypsy's Lane joined the main road. Coalman Haines took a small paper bag of flour from the sack he kept in the pantry, and Adam took the flour to Singer.

'I've seen this caper at the White Hart,' Tustin said, as Singer floured his face and put on the look of a very sick man. The Norton team thought that the rain was a blessing after all if Singer was to entertain, and sixty-seven runs would not have been a big score for Ayshon to beat. Singer stood on the wooden chest which held the home team's cricket gear. He looked quite pathetic as he sang:

My life's one long list of complaints commencing at my birth.
I've paid away in doctors' bills enough to buy the earth,
There's scarcely any ailment that I can boast of having missed,
You will agree, I'm sure with me, when you have heard my list.
Ague, diabetes, measles and the croup
With warm blains and chilblains and coughs that make me whoop,
Rheumatics, mathematics, ping-pong and catarrh,
With diabolic, painter's colic, gout and roume var;
Happy plexy, dismal plexy, biles that give me beans,
'Tis bound to happen, yet it is, to those who don't eat greens;
With sunstroke, daughter stroke, sciatica and twins . . .

He went on from here for nearly two minutes. Then young

Charlie Cambridge, Jim Cambridge's boy, who had come to learn farming, gave a few songs and recitations.

After the impromptu concert in the railway carriage, some of the Ayshon players joined with some from Norton at the White Hart Inn. The Norton men had come over in a two horse brake driven by Jonathan Davis, the village blacksmith. He stabled the horses at the White Hart.

In the bar where the spiked cricket boots moved the sawdust, Bert Chandler sat in his usual place near the spitoon. He had a knack of sizing up all the fellows as they came through the front door; Tustin Finch, Jones the under carter, Arthur Jackson, young Charlie Cambridge and Ruby Bushell. The farm men usually drank cider but on this occasion Ruby Bushell treated the home team and the visitors to beer.

Singer Sallis gave Bert a meaningful look as the men settled down to their drink. 'Another black sovereign, Bert,' he said.

Bert knew exactly what was meant, he knew that Ruby had been left money by his mother after her death two years before. These sovereigns had been hoarded by Jane Bushell and kept in an old oak chest. No one knew how many, but there were hundreds of coins which went black from being kept out of circulation so long.

'As black as the ace of spades,' Bert remarked and added that if only Jane knew how the money was being sent down the drain, she would turn in her grave. 'Drink gets the better of Ruby,' he said, 'makes him foolhardy and there be plenty of his cronies around who help him to spend the money.'

Tom Bowman came into the pub and eyebrows were raised. 'Selling the *War Cry*, Tom?' Ruby called from his seat where he appeared to be chairing a meeting of cricketers from both Norton and Ashton. Tom smiled and Singer Sallis, knowing what drink to offer him, handed him a glass of stone ginger beer which he poured from a stone bottle. Turning to Tom, Bert Chandler said, 'I suppose you know I be supposed to retire at Michaelmas and me and Fanny ull have to live on the Lloyd George.'

Tom replied, 'You have had a good innings, been careful I reckon.'

The old shepherd drew his chair up to Tom Bowman saying, 'Keep it under yer hat but we've saved a couple of hundred pound and Mr. Bushell's gwain to give me a pension of seven bob a wick.'

'Whose going to be shepherd at Michaelmas?' Tom inquired.

The answer came in a whisper, 'That crater as have just changed one of his old mother's sovereigns.' The shepherd then explained to Tom how that he had tried hard to teach Ruby the art of shepherding. He said that young Ruby could make a good shepherd if he put his mind to it, but that he kept the wrong company. Bert Chandler seemed to want to tell someone in confidence of his young master's stupidity.

'It's shameful that Fred Bushell's son should be such a fool,' he said. He then told Tom of some of the things Ruby had done, like releasing old Harry Havelod's fox that he kept chained to a kennel by his cot when the hounds met at the Manor. 'Caught the poor dumb animal up Cotton's Lane they did. He only ran about a quarter of a mile and the Master of the Hunt, Lord Coventry, wasn't very pleased when they caught a fox with a collar on.'

He told of the night in February when Ruby and Tustin rang the church bells at two in the morning after a night on the drink; how Ruby and one of his Cheltenham cronies raced their horses by moonlight from the Manor to Beckford Inn and unhung the farm gates all the way to Grafton, letting Frank Bishop's cattle into the road. 'Ah, he's allus bin a rodney,' Bert Chandler said with a sigh. 'Ever since he put Durgin's cat in the ferret box along of that big fitcher ferret that we used to use as a liner.'

'What happened to the cat, then?' Tom Bowman said looking so worried, for Tom loved his cats, and thought of the time when he lived with his mother, Mary Ann, in the cottage next to the White Hart and Farmer John shot their cats for a pastime when they strayed in the field at the back.

'The cat killed the ferret. That's a licker unt it?' the shepherd replied.

'Perhaps marriage to Mildred Churchway, the station master at Landsdown's daughter, will steady him,' Tom offered, trying to console the old shepherd. Tustin came up to them at that. 'Postponed, they say the wedding is, to July,' he said with a grin.

'Ah,' Bert replied, 'she's got many admirers, and look at the state our gaffer's son is in tonight.'

The station master at Landsdown Cheltenham Midland had long been worried about his beautiful daughter, though he was reassured by the fact that some years' experience in nursing meant she was not naive like many girls of her generation. Mildred used to cut a pretty picture at the Boxing Day meet of the Cotswold hounds at the Queen's Hotel when the pack drew Queen's Wood. She rode a fast hunter alongside Ruby on his liver chestnut cob. But they often parted before the end of the day. Ruby found the company at the King's Arms at Prestbury too good to leave after a refresher. So Mildred would hack home with one of the followers, Percy, a smart dark chap who farmed under Bredon. It's said that Percy was rarely at the kill, but more often gone to cover with Mildred or some other lass. Their horses could be seen from the Vale as the light faded, tied to a tree on the brow of the hill as they made music together on the beech leaves in Fiddler's Nap.

When she came to Ayshon by train, Ruby would meet her at the station with the pony and trap. But often before the sun left the Vale and sank beneath the Malvern Hills on those Saturday nights Ruby was prostrate with drink, a condition old Fanny Chandler called, 'Prostitute with drink.' Leaving the sofa at the Manor after a session with Mildred, Ruby would stagger to the stable for the cob. 'Just sit there on the bench man and leave it to me,' Mildred used to say as she harnessed the cob and backed it into the governess cart. Ruby stumbled aboard, Mildred took the reins, driving like some twentieth-century Boadicea the eleven miles to Cheltenham.

Jim Cambridge came into the White Hart with Ralph who had met him off the seven o'clock Birmingham train. 'Have you a good memory, sir?' Bert Chandler asked Mr. Cambridge.

'Yes, I have, Bert,' was the reply.

'Can you recollect, sir?' Joe asked.

'The same thing that is, Bert,' was the reply of the iron and steel merchant.

Bert shook his head then said, 'Do you remember borrowing a dibber off me awhile back to plant the cabbage plants?'

'Yes, I do Joe, very well,' he answered.

'Do you recollect ever bring it back?' Joe went on.

'No, I don't,' was the honest reply. Jim laughed, and agreed that sometimes memory and recollection are different. 'Give Bert a drink on me landlord.' Turning to Singer Sallis, Jim Cambridge said, 'I gather Bert left school at thirteen years old. Bredon Hill has given him a real education.'

When Harry Carter drove over from Evesham the following week, he and Tom Bowman walked up Bredon one evening after the men had finished work. Durgin Green, Jack Gardener and Alf Miller had given the sprout plants by Great Hill Barn a second hoeing and young Adam had been borrowed for a week off Fred Bushell to horse hoe in between the rows. The charlock lay withered in the May sun where Adam and Noble had worked with the horse hoe or skim plough.

Old Bert Chandler came from behind the row of fir trees with his dog, Rosie. He had been having a last look at his ewes and lambs in the cool of the evening (a good time to notice the lamb struck with the blowing fly). 'Working late ay, Bert?' Harry Carter said as the partners met the shepherd.

'Ah, we shepherds don't work with the clock like the day men, the yows and lambs must be looked after.'

'Bad job about the first cricket match being spoiled by that storm,' Harry said.

Bert Chandler stopped in the gateway near the remains of the sainfoin rick, placed his arms on the top rail of the gate and said quietly to Rosie, 'Sit down ull ya. Been a bad wick, my bwoys. Not enough rain for the crops, I suppose, and the greens are looking sick in Evesham.'

'But our sprouts look kind by the barn, don't they, Tom?' Harry said.

'Yes,' Tom Bowman replied. 'There is no doubt the stones up here hold the damp and now we understand why some hill farmers never cart away the stones off the hill but send their men with hammers to break them small enough for them to pass between their corn drills.'

'What's gone wrong this week then, Tom?' Harry said as he broke the breech of his gun in the gateway. 'Lost any sheep?' he added.

'No. To start off with a gypsy tackled our parson as he went home from church with the collection down Rabbit Lane.' The shepherd then described how Reverend Rushton, who won his boxing blue at Oxford, knocked the gypsy into the ditch near the sandpit, but not before the parson had been given a black eye. 'He's stopped in now for the rest of the wick with a piece of beefsteak plastered over his one eye. Master Bushell says it's a beauty,' the shepherd said.

Tom Bowman said he was sorry to hear of Fred Bushell's trouble with his bull.

'What happened?' Harry from Evesham asked.

Bert Chandler replied, 'Now ya know I got a lot of time for young Tustin Finch. He's a gallus young devil, always up to mischief egged on by Ruby. But as a stockman he's a nineter. If the cows was his own they udn't be looked after better. But he's so careless, allus got his yud full of some foolhardy when his mind should be elsewhere.

'That thur bull o Fred's, Joker, come out of Grammy, a pure Hereford, time and time again I've told Tustin to put a leather washer on the chog chain over the tie as fastens it. Monday night, damn me, if Joker didn't get out in the village to Arthur Jackson's field by the wood and gored a bullock of Arthur's to death. Course, our gaffer paid Arthur compensation, but Arthur stuck the beast and bled him. I skinned and dressed it and by all accounts our gaffer's gwain to divide the meat that's uttable among the poor. Young Adam took Noble up to the ood uth a trace hoss and they rolled the beast on to a gate, then dragged um down to the farm.

'And thee should'st 'ave sin the hoss a capering and rearing when he smelt the blood. Mind that, Master Harry, Noble a sin some sights out thur among the Boers. Hosses be real funny when they smells blood. Ast ever thee had any trouble when you sows dried blood among the gardening crops? I've sin a drove a cows sniff the air and turn back along the road when blood and bone meal is being broadcast on the ground. 'Tis natural, Master Harry, 'cos they smells their own kind as bin ground up as casualty animals by the like of the knacker men at Gloucester.'

'Who caught the bull?' Harry asked.

'Didn't take no catching 'cos he dropped his nose ring over the arrowhead railings outside the garden of that widow's house at Middle Farm.'

Walking down Bredon together Tom and Harry and the shepherd parted at Paris Gardens where the shepherd made his way to his cottage and the other men walked to Mr. Bushell's house at Grafton. Fred Bushell was busy in his garden putting some barley straw under the trusses of blossom on his strawberries. The strawberries, Harry remarked, were as good as he had seen even among the market gardeners of Donnybrook.

'It's the muck from the stable that has held them this year of drought, Harry. Bert Chandler dug it in last winter on Saturday afternoons,' Fred Bushell replied.

'Bad job about your bull,' Tom said. 'Your shepherd told us about in on the hill.'

'Yes, Tom, but he's a good stock getter and I've got a young one by him out of a Hereford cow that'll suit you when Harry and you start a dairy,' was Fred's reply. Then he asked Harry, 'How's the sprouts looking on the hill? You're the expert in these matters.'

'Capital, Master Bushell, so different from the crops in the Vale and that animal oil Durgin put on the binder twine around the headland kept the rabbits back. There's hardly any damage from them. And how much do we owe you for Adam and the horse hoeing last week?'

Fred Bushell straightened his back, lit his pipe and said, 'Come on into the cool of the dairy. Now then, Adam's wages are now eight shillings a week and I charge five shillings a day for the horse, so that's one pound eighteen shillings.'

Harry whipped two pounds out of his pocket saying, 'Give Adam a couple of bob please, he's made a clinking job up there.'

Fred Bushell drew a pint of cider from the barrel for himself then he took two bottles of stone ginger beer from the shelf and poured out two glasses for his tenants. 'Your man, Durgin, has started farming in Hill Withy,' Fred Bushell said with a laugh, adding, 'well he's got an acre of allotments off the Railway Company. I put in a word for him as my land adjoins the small holdings. You see Tiddley Pond from Beckford is crocked up with rheumatism and was giving the land up, so Durgin will join Dick, Joe, Frank and Jack down on the Company's grounds.'

'Lucky man, Durgin is,' Harry replied, 'going into an acre planted with peas, strawberries and a nice patch of wheat.'

'Was Bert Chandler still on the hill when you were there after tea, Harry? He's a man I'll miss at Michaelmas, but Ruby is to take over then. I can't see him shepherding all hours like Tom, though.'

'He looks after your sheep as if they were his own, I reckon,' Tom said to the farmer.

'By the way, have you fellows had an invitation to Ruby's wedding. It's July now, in Cheltenham. You'll be getting one, I'd like you to be there when he marries Mildred.' Harry said they would be glad to accept and wondered whether Ruby's future father-in-law had told Mr. Bushell about the vacant plot at Hill Withy. Fred Bushell said that he was generally in the know on such matters.

Hill Withy was a plot of land split in two by the railway in 1864, and then let by the Company to smallholders. In this way, when the Midland Railway were obliged to buy whole fields for their track to run through they were able to supply a growing need for smallholding by renting the land to villagers. One sees the awkward shaped pieces of land dug and planted by such men. Plots which the adjoining landowners could not be bothered to rent and add to their farms were skillfully tilled by smallholders.

Fred Bushell had several fields adjoining the line which he grazed with young horses to get them used to the smoke, the steam and the noise of passing trains, so that when they were taken to the station to load or unload from the siding they were not so frightened by the black smoke-belching monsters of the iron road.

Fred was fast becoming a lover of poetry, a deep thinker in his old age. His times at market were less often, but he liked the things of nature; his garden, his bees, the church, talking to the parson. An old parson, long since gone, was his favourite, the Dorset poet. He loved William Barnes and the piece he wrote about the spring always a favourite time of the year at the house in Grafton.

THE SPRING

When wintry weather's all a'done
An' brooks do sparkle in the zun
An' naisy building rooks do vlee
Wi' sticks towards their elm tree.
When birds do sing and we can zee
Upon the boughs the buds of spring,
Then I'm as happy as a king
A-vield wi' health an' zunsheen.

Vor then the cowslip's hanging flower
A-wetted in the zunny shower

Do grow with vi'lets sweet o'smell
Beside the wood-screen'd greagle's bell
Where drushes eggs wi' shy blue shell
Do lie in mossy nest among
The thorns while they do zing their zong
At evenen in the zunsheen.

An' God do make his win' to blow
An' rain do vall vor high an' low
An' bid his mornen zun to rest
Vor all alike an' groun' an'skies
Ha colours vor the poor man's eyes.
An' in our trials He is near
To hear our moan an zee our tear,
An' turn our clouds to zunsheen.

An' many times when I do vind
Things all goo wrong an' voh unkind.
To see the happy veeden herds
An' hear the zinging o' the birds.
Do soothe my sorrow more than words
Vor I do zee that 'tis our sin
Do macke woones soul so dark ithin
When God would gie woone zunsheen.

'You mentioned a young bull that you would sell to us, Mr.
Bushell,' Harry said as the three men walked through the garden at
Grafton where beehives of plaited straw lined the path between the
fruit trees. Tom was interested in the bees and he remembered the
hives he had at Klondike field in Donnybrook and selling the honey
to Mr. Elliot the chemist at four pence a pound.

'Ah Harry, he will be ready for service in a month or so. How
many cows do you expect to have in your dairy at Lower Farm?'

'Twenty, but Tom will buy the cows and the bull and there are
several folk in the village with a couple of cows who make butter.
They can bring them to our bull.'

Harry then said that his chief interest in the land was the growing
of market garden produce for the markets of the north of England.

Tom placed his hand on Mr. Bushell's shoulder saying. 'Harry's the man who'll show the folk around Bredon Hill how to grow Telegraph peas with pods like broad beans. He can bundle a hundred buds of asparagus as well as anyone I know, and we have selected seeds of early wallflowers in my back kitchen which Harry can bring to bloom in March. Some of the land sick with corn from your last tenant will bud and bloom, and I promise your land will be a picture.'

It was dusk when Harry and Tom approached Stanley Farm. The rabbits were grazing the short grass near the moat pond and Harry was tempted to use his gun but said, 'No good, Tom, now, 'cos the does will be in kindle and the bucks will eat strong from the oven.'

At the top of Gypsy's Lane, Durgin Green pushed a flat bedded wheelbarrow loaded from Hill Withy with the produce planted by Tiddley Pond. A rope was slung over his shoulders from the wheelbarrow's handles to take some of the weight off his arms.

'Inions,' Harry said with a smile, that being the Evesham brogue for onions.

'Oi Master, they be Lesbons. I've washed them in Carrants Brook and the Missus is gwain to bunch them for market,' he replied. 'I still do a good day's work for you two gaffers though, and I hope you don't think I reserves my energy for the 'lotment.'

'We think nothing of the kind, Durgin,' Tom said. 'We aren't so stupid to deny a working man like you his allotment, like it was when your Dad had to be satisfied with just a couple of rows of potatoes on the farm headland.'

In the farm house kitchen Harry and Tom had supper together before going to bed. Harry had told Alice, his wife, that he would stay overnight at Stanley Farm ready for work in the early morning. He walked across the yard into the barn where Tom's hens perched along the hay rack, the light of his lantern shone on the white Leghorns and his cob, Dick, whinnied at the sight of his master.

He thought, next year I'll have more hens than Tom when I leave Donnybrook and come to the Lower Farm, and ducks in the thatched duck pen, they can swim on the moat pond. His thoughts went to the wild life on Bredon—the partridges, the rabbits and hares, and the growing parsley planted to attract the hares. In his mind's eye he saw the row of ferret boxes in the yard. I'll fill them and breed some of the finest fitcher ferrets that ever hunted on Bredon.

In Walnut Tree Cottage, Durgin and Annie Green sat in the wash house in the light of an oil lamp and tied onions for market. The bunches of white and green salad onions were given their final wash in a bath of water drawn from Durgin's well and after Durgin had bundled the bunches with withy twigs in dozens, he carefully filled a couple of market hampers.

Annie Green had, since her disappointment in failing to have a family, opened a little shop. She sold home-made chocolate, made by an old recipe using cocoa butter. She collected the empty Camp Coffee bottles from the farm cottages and filled them with home brewed ginger and herb beer. The corks were tied with pudding string to keep in the fermented drink, a drink relished by the farm men of the Bredon Hill village. In the wash house where the copper boiler brewed the so-called pop, the shelves were lined with large coffee bottles ready for sale.

Old Durgin collected dandelions, nettles and other herbs to make the brew, a drink strongly tasting of ginger. On autumn evenings Durgin picked the large ketchup mushrooms off Bredon for Annie to make ketchup for sale. The mushrooms on the hill were famous for their massive size. Annie Green's speciality was raspberry vinegar used by the villagers to flavour the Sunday dinnertime Yorkshire pudding.

However, there was one drink which Durgin and Annie used themselves and for friends who called in. It was never sold. Bee wine, a fairly common drink enjoyed by the Bredon Hill villagers, was a mysterious concoction which fermented in a glass container on the cottage windowsill. No one seemed to know how bee wine was made. The fact that it was such a mystery rendered it a luxury. A kind of manna-like substance was put from a packet into clear water and fed, fed with sugar which made the so called bees work up and down in the glass jar as if they were some sort of tadpole. After so long the liquid was strained and bottled. Durgin and Annie drank the wine before bedtime under the ingle in their cottage sitting room.

'Durgin has broke the pledge now he and Annie drink wine at night,' Tustin said to Alf and Jack as the four men were standing near the village cross after Alf and Jack had been to Annie's to fetch a bagful of herb beer in the coffee bottles.

'Surprised I be of you, Durgin,' Tustin teased. 'A strong chapel man and so called teetotal, slyly swigging wine in the cottage.'

Durgin, always ready for Tustin's onslaughts, replied, ' 'Tis non-alcoholic and you know it, like the pop we sell. I'll show you the packet that the bees come in.' The little old man walked to his door, picked up an empty packet and showed the men. 'There,' he said, 'now bist satisfied you, jumping senseless torrel, Tustin.'

I've always admired Durgin's sincerity when, as a very old widower after Annie's death, he still drank bee wine and insisted that he was teetotal, but the bees I believe, were some kind of yeast which fermented with the sugar to make a mead as sweet as nectar.

As the month of May ended Durgin found a real delight in the new allotment where he could work in the evening beside Dick, Frank, Jack and old Joe. Joe Green lived alone on the hill; a wise man, a man who could forecast the seasons and he and Durgin could converse about the natural things and the Sunday sermon where they both attended chapel. The Seville beans planted in Hill Withy by Tiddley Pond were in flower. Durgin cut the top off the plants with a hook and looked forward to the dinners with the new potatoes in June. His wheat, a crop of Squareheads Master, stood well in green ear.

Joe, a pensioner, an old soldier, agreed to cut the half acre with hook and crook, to bind and stook for Durgin in August. Adam, with Noble his favourite horse, walked the long rows of mangolds and swede holding the tails of Mr. Bushell's horse hoe. Mr. Bushell knew if the rains never came all the summer, his mangolds would grow fast in the sun feeding on the yard muck of last autumn.

May 29th is celebrated by the folk who live under Bredon Hill as Oak Apple Day, the anniversary of the Restoration of Charles II in 1660 and to remember his great escape after the battle of Worcester. Charles hid during his flight in an oak tree at Boscobel in Shropshire climbing the tree with a henroost ladder. A man called Moore, a villager of Kersoe, which lies between Elmley Castle and Ayshon, was said to have helped Charles escape from Worcester after the battle. Mr. Moore was visiting the city taking a waggon load of hay there with his two horse team. The Parliamentarians were pursuing

Charles and Moore, seeing the King's plight, pulled his horses and waggon across the road blocking it from the troops.

Fred Bushell whose father-in-law, old Nehemiah, farmed in Elmley, always drove over to his neighbouring village to see the school children in procession and dancing around a Maypole on Oak Apple Day. Dressed in their Sunday clothes and wearing the oak leaves with the Maytime oak apples hanging from the twigs, they made a colourful sight on that May morning.

6

Barnaby Bright

JUNE 11TH, THE FEAST OF SAINT BARNABAS, IS MARKED IN the old almanac by the sign of a rake denoting the beginning of hay harvest. The proverb says, 'On Saint Barnabas put the scythe to the grass.' Glastonbury, noted for the Holy Thorn which grew in the Abbey churchyard, once also had a miraculous walnut tree which never budded until the feast of St. Barnabas, then on June 11th shot forth its leaves and flourished. This tree was mentioned in the metrical life of Joseph of Arimathea in 1520.

> Great meruaylles [marvels] men may se at Glastenbury,
> One of a walnut tree that there doth stande
> In the holy grounde called the semetery
> Hard by ye place where Kynge Arthur was foude
> South fro Josephs Chapel it is walled in roude.
> It bereth no leaves tyll the day of Saynt Barnabe
> And than that tree that standeth in the grounde
> Sproteth his leaves as fayre as any other tree.

June the 11th in the old calendar was Midsummer Day, so the proverb came, 'Barnaby Bright, Barnaby Bright, the longest day and the shortest night.' Barnaby bright is the popular name for the ladybird, an insect very common about this time of the year.

In early June 1911 Fred Bushell bought a new Bomford mowing machine from Mr. Meats in Cheltenham. The signal red pole shaft and wooden suppletrees made a vivid contrast to the bright canary yellow wheels and iron seat. The machine came in a truck to the station and young Adam Hunt, together with Jones the under carter, unloaded it into the heavy dray to bring it to the Manor rickyard, where Bert Chandler helped to take it off the dray, wheeling it down a couple of planks.

The haymaking on Bushell's farm began by the mowing on 11th June or, if that day fell on a Sunday, the cutting of the first swath would be on the 12th. Fred still studied the ways of his ancestors who farmed under Bredon Hill before the new calendar came into being in the mid-eighteenth century. Old Midsummer he called that June day and by starting the grass mowing then he hoped to finish his hay by St. Swithin's or Apple Christening Day on July 15th.

Bert Chandler had mown the Manor Farm hay fields with an old machine ever since his father worked with a scythe alongside Tom Bowman's father. Fred Bushell insisted that either he or Adam's father were in the same field as the machine just in case there was an accident, for a nest of angry wasps could cause the horses to run away and unseat the driver, or Bert Chandler might cut himself while sharpening a mower knife. 'Get the horses in early in the morning, about half past four, Adam,' Fred said to his newest young under carter.

Noble, Merriman, Prince, Pleasant and Blackbird came down in a line head to tail, haltered, to the stable from the meadow below the Paris Gardens known as Boss Close. Adam led Noble in front, while Tustin walked behind followed by his cattle dog. The morning sun rose over Broadway Hill and the lush grass under the apple trees in the orchard soaked the boots of the men with dew, a dew which soon went when the sun was what Bert Chandler called as high as Sedgeberrow church spire.

' 'Twill be a brawmer today, you, agun,' Tustin muttered in the harness room between swigs of cider from his costrel bottle.

'Who's gwain to ride the mower this year, now Bert Chandler's legs be rheumaticy?' asked Adam.

'You bwoy, so Ruby reckons. He's gwain to get married soon, then going to Bournemouth honeymooning with Mildred,' Tustin replied.

'Why was the wedding postponed?' Adam asked meekly.

'Ah, one day you ull understand about women; there's times they be at their peak, so to speak, while at other times they be off colour.' Tustin laughed with his usual horsey laugh. 'Thee hast to hold the candle to women whey they beunt up to the mark.'

Fred Bushell came through the gate from his garden into the yard. Tustin put the bottle down saying, 'Yer comes the gaffer,' as the gate slammed to after him.

'Gear up Noble and Merriman, they are pretty quiet horses to pull the machine,' he said to man and boy.

The light leather-covered Army surplus steel traces with the looped backbands were hooked into the harness and strapped to the horses' collars. Fred Bushell brought with him a pair of rope G.O. reins new from Ernie Hines' saddler's shop and gave them to Adam. 'Here, these are soft to the hands my boy, the white cotton variety, they won't make your hands sore.'

'Am I to ride the machine then, Master?' Adam said, a little nervously.

'When I've showed you how to mow. I'll see you are all right, and you, Tustin, when you have seen to the cows you are to help keeping the knives of the mower sharp for Adam, and raking out the swath from the hedge bottom,' was the reply.

In Didcot Ham, bordered by the branch railway line on one side and Carrants Brook on the other, the grass stood a fair crop considering the drought. Mr. Bushell and Adam hooked the horses on the machine. 'Now see that the mower is always out of gear when you are oiling it, Adam,' the Master of the Manor said.

With a long spouted can he then squirted oil along the mower knife between the finger, then he oiled the driving bar and checked to see that the reservoir at the back where the cogs drove the knife from the wheels was full of oil. Merriman and Noble had been used to the clatter of the old mowing machine with Tom. Fred Bushell mounted the seat, took the reins, stooped down and put the gear into the 'on' position, quietly called, 'Cup Merriman, cup Noble.' The knife chattered, the machine moved forward, leaving behind a swath of green grass, clover and buttercup in a neat row alongside the edge of the brook. Adam took a rake and waited until his master had been around the field three times, then he started raking the swath from under the hedge and by the brook making two swaths into one so that the mower could be worked around the field in the opposite direction to mow the swath on the edge of the field.

'Adam,' Fred Bushell called as he stopped his horses under the red withy tree by Gypsy's Lane. 'Come here and take over.'

As Adam mounted the machine, Fred Bushell impressed on him again to keep his mower well oiled, to always put it out of gear when he dismounted, to see that the knife was always sharp. At this moment Tustin arrived.

'You won't need me here, Master, now Adam's going to mow, ull ya?'

'Of course,' Fred replied. 'This machine is very sensitive, highly geared from the wheels which drive the cogs and from the cogs to the knife. When a horse just snatches to move a fly from his front leg, the knife will start and agitate.' Adam looked worried. 'No need to worry boy, Tustin is here to look after things. If the mowing grass clogs the knife, just put the machine out of gear and Tustin can rake it away.' A knife stand under the withies was there for Tustin to clamp the spare knife to and sharpen it with a file. 'It's a young man's job with a machine, Adam. Away you go, boy.'

'Cup Noble, cup Merriman,' the boy said nervously, and soon he was carried away by the movement of horse and mower, seeing the grass fall slain before the knife. The brown stubble, the cracked ground underneath, was patterned in the rows between the cut grass.

'Just keep an eye on him, Tustin, you see he has a good hand with the reins. Walk around the field and look for wasps nests, take this scythe and cut around them if you find any.'

'There is a partridge nest anant the chestnut tree by the railroad,' Tustin replied.

'Cut a swath around the sitting bird and leave enough cover for her, then Adam can steer his horses away from the nest,' Fred replied.

The heat of the sun that June day was merciless so that at one o'clock Fred Bushell walked down Gypsy's Lane and saw that Adam had broken the back of the field leaving only a couple of acres unmown. The horse flies were doing their worst, sucking blood from the broad chests of Noble and Merriman. Tustin put elder flowers laced in the bridles to ward off the insects from where they settled round the horses' eyes and noses, as Tustin said, 'Like the brown flies on a cow's turd.'

'I say, Adam, whoa, come here a minute,' his master said. Noble's long tail switched at the flies, sometimes trapping the rope rein held in Adam's hand so tightly under the crupper that he or Tustin had to lift the tail to retrieve the rein. 'Adam you've done well for a youngster, unhitch the horses, take them in the cool of the stable, don't let them drink too long at the water trough and have your dinner. Now Tustin, you and Adam make a staddle nine yards by five under the big walnut tree where we had the rick last year. Take old Pleasant in the dray and fetch some boltings of straw from the straw rick and make a good bottom for the hay rick.'

'What about this grass as yunt cut, sir?' Adam asked.

'In the cool of the evening bring Prince and Pleasant down here and you should finish the field comfortable by the edge of night. You'll find the grass mows better when the dew rises,' Fred replied.

While Adam and Tustin finished the mowing grass in Didcot Ham and the young rabbits scurried off to the railway batter where the scrubby hawthorn bushes gave cover, Bert Chandler sipped the cider in the cool of Singer Sallis's bar. He stood with Arthur Jackson, that dog and stick farmer from the Wood.

'I see Master Bushell's mower going around the Ham early this morning when I was maggoting my ewes on Cank's Bank. Who's riding the machine this year, Bert?'

This question of Arthur's made Bert think awhile before he gave an answer, for he knew that for some many years the meadows had been his province on the early mornings in June where he cut the swaths at haymaking. He didn't like to think that he was getting past it.

In fact, those early mornings when the dew lay wet by the brook and the village was asleep and he had worked with only the birds and the rabbits and his horses for company were times when his mind went back to the mowing team with scythes. His father, William Bowman, Spider Watchet, and Long Fred, all with backs bent, skimming what was known as the Dismal, under the ryegrass, cockfoot, Timothy clover and wild vetches, and seeing the wilted swath lie changing colour in the sun. Just the switch of the scythe, not the clatter of the horse mower in those days when Queen Victoria had her two Jubilees.

'Young Adam Hunt is riding the machine this year, Arthur, and 'tis a good year for a bwoy to start. The crops be thin, owing to the drought. I've known the time when the grass was as high as the hosses' shoulders and ud reve in front of the knife. I was forever

getting down off the seat and forking a one side. The brook
meadows be lush,' Bert added.

Arthur smiled as he said, 'Never mind, Bert, you'll be umpiring
for us in the Broadenham on Saturday.'

'Now that's a job I can manage to a nicety Arthur, but 'tis a rough
road to Dublin on the iron seat of a machine this year when the
ground is chauned in cracks that the stale of my crook ull hardly
bottom. Then there's my piles, plagues me summat cruel, and me
double rupture.'

Arthur passed his tobacco tin to shepherd Bert who filled his clay
pipe, sending the blue smoke up amongst the black beams in Singer's
kitchen. 'I remember your old Dad helping to cut the brook
meadows when I was at school, and recall what happened when the
first mowing machine came into the parish when some of the old
men stuck iron harrow tines upright among the grass to break the
knife of the machine. Oi, they were jealous of their jobs then a day,
Bert.'

'Yes,' Bert replied, 'I remember old William Bowman, a rum fella
when he had drunk a pint of his parsnip wine. They drank it like cider
on wet days in the hovel, he and Reverend Harrison. Now young
Tom Bowman along of Harry Carter has got a clinking crop of
sprouts on our gaffer's field on Bredon Hill, and that's the only bit a
green to be seen for miles.'

Arthur opened the door of the White Hart where his dog lay
panting under the wall after a day among the gorse at the Wood
Farm. 'Come on Bert, it's getting dusk and I've got to shut the fowls
and the geese up in case Reynard gives us a visit.'

Bert Chandler walked from the inn and was soon back at his
cottage with Fanny where he lay on the flock mattress on the big
brass bedstead under the open window.

Arthur Jackson's homeward journey through the wood was by
way of a ride between the young larches and that fox and badger
infested scrub land known as Cank's Bank. His dog at heel was so
used to such journeys he ignored the hordes of young rabbits that
cheekily stayed clipping the greenery on the well worn path until
man and dog were only a few yards away. Arthur was unmoved
when a couple of deer from Elmley Park sprinted from the larches to
Cank's Bank.

Then a nightingale sang from the sallow willow bed by the stream. Arthur stood still a minute and cast his eyes in the direction of the stream but the light was almost gone. He did see from the hill the wisps of smoke from the cottage chimneys and picked out Bert Chandler's chimney near the church tower.

Arthur mused in his restricted way. His uneducated mind told him that he was witnessing a pageant of the sights and sounds that few people could enjoy, a show which was enacted every twilight, seen and heard by shepherds, gamekeepers and lovers, perhaps. How grand was the feel of it all. The moon rising over the Cotswold edge, the dim outline of larches, elder bushes heavy with cream blossom, giving an almost intoxicating scent. The white tails of moonlit rabbits, the grunt of badgers and the pathetic call of dog foxes.

Arthur lit his pipe, sauntered on until he reached the Heaver, a rough-hewn hingeless gate made by old Oliver, the travelling rough carpenter of Bredon Hill. From here he saw the smoke of his own chimney. As he walked through the little orchard past the pump over the well, the oil lamp shone through the stone mullioned window of the living room. Mrs. Jackson sat by the great white scrubbed table mending children's clothes.

'A regular job this is, Arthur,' she said, 'mending the torn dresses and jackets of our Frank, Ethel and Richard.'

Arthur cut a slice of cheese from the chunk on the table, then with a little twist broke the top off a cottage loaf and put it on a plate. From an earthenware jar he stabbed at the pickles with his fork, bringing out onions, cauliflower, red cabbage and gherkins. 'Have you had supper, Mother?' he said.

'Ay, I had a little with the youngsters afore they went to bed,' was the reply.

'Sorry about the state of their clothes,' he ventured. 'But 'tis the brambles on the hill. They are in bloom now, but you know the blackberry harvest in September brings us in a good many coppers.'

Mrs. Jackson sighed saying, 'I suppose the boys are useful now a day bringing in the cows from among the gorse and briar for the milking, then looking up the eggs. Many in the White Hart?' she added.

'Bert Chandler was there and was a bit upset about being unable to do Fred Bushell's mowing,' Arthur replied, 'and I've got a bottle of stout for you, Mother.'

Mrs. Jackson nodded, put down the sewing and poured herself a drink into a cider cup from the mantelpiece. As they mounted the stairs together Arthur said with a laugh, 'It's the Club Feast on Monday at the White Hart. You'll be coming, Mother? We'll have a day for the new King.'

Arthur's wife held the candle towards the almanac over the bed saying, 'Ah, 'tis Trinity Monday next week. That's Club Day, always was. I'll be there, it does make a change from being up here away from my family in the village.'

As Arthur got into bed he slipped an arm around his wife saying quietly, 'We got a nice little holding up here, independent like.'

'Now Arthur, careful boy, you know what Doctor Overthrow always says. He can date most of the births in the village back to either Ayshon Club or Dumbleton Flower Show when the men have been on the drink.'

Trinity Monday, the week following Whitsun had been the official day for the Club Feast at Ayshon since the Benefit Society was started by Thomas Packer of Cheltenham in 1876, the year Tom Bowman was born. Mr. Packer started the Society in conjunction with the Ayshon doctor, Edward Overthrow. Conservative in origin, the Club members wore blue rosettes while the horses which brought supporters from Cheltenham were decked with blue ribbons. Packer was a great lover of Bredon Hill and he wrote a book entitled, *Round Bredon Hill*, describing the place and its people.

Ayshon villagers strongly supported their Society, paying in their subscriptions every Friday night to Singer Sallis at the White Hart pub. In 1911 when Adam Hunt was only thirteen years old he was eligible to join and, having joined at Christmas, was entitled to attend the Club Day celebrations which started with a service at St. Barbara's church at nine o'clock.

Alderton brass band arrived just before nine. Fred Bushell had sent Adam and Tustin over to the village fetching the bandsmen and their instruments on farm drays pulled by Fred's horses. On that day Fred Bushell's horses' coats shone like silk, the harness gleamed, and the brasses glittered in the morning sun. At the church, Reverend

Rushton, that benevolent parson, met the members. They marched from the village cross, where they assembled, up the churchyard past the drooping ash trees and the big beech tree where the leaves shone like polished mahogany.

In fact everything shone that day. Every member carried a wooden staff, either nut or ash with a brass emblem mounted at the top. The Club flag was a feature remembered by the folk for years. It was hung from a long pole and carried by the tallest and strongest member. The church service was short and simple for Reverend Rushton didn't believe in keeping folk cooped up while he sermonised on such summer's day — a day to remember when holidays were few.

After church the uniformed Alderton band struck up 'Rule Brittania' and the slow march up the village street began. It had to be slow as the procession stopped outside all the farm houses where the jugs of beer and cider awaited all and sundry to help themselves. The jugs were standing on garden walls, on the top of stand pipes, on the steps of houses.

In the yard of the White Hart stood a large marquee where the meal had been prepared by Singer Sallis and his helpers. Singer Sallis had been told every year by Mr. Bushell and Doctor Overthrow to put on the best meal possible for the members. If the money left over from Sick Benefits paid out during the year was not sufficient, they agreed to pay Singer the difference. What a spread there was that Coronation year. The joints of beef and the cooked hams, the gooseberry pies were relished by the men off the land. The doctor was in the chair at the top table supported by Fred Bushell and Reverend Rushton. When everyone had eaten and had drunk as much as they could, the doctor said, 'Does anyone want any more?'

After a few seconds silence, Ruby Bushell stood up as well as he could on his drink-weakened legs and said, 'Yes, I do.' The gathering were stunned for a few seconds, then Ruby shouted, 'Tomorrow,' amid laughter.

After the feast a small committee had arranged sports in the Little Piece. Here blindfolded men raced with passengers in wheelbarrows. The stream off the hill ran alongside the field by the footpath and many of the racers finished up in the stream. Large iron quoits were tossed at the pin from a distance on Singer's rink alongside his pub. The target pin stood on a cheese of puddled clay and was watered to keep it tacky. As men threw, the bystanders called out in horse language according to where the quoit fell: 'Ett a bit, aw a bit, comey back, gee back!' Such a rural scene enacted by their grandfathers before them entertained the men of 1911.

Fred Bushell gave a pig, a weaner of eight-weeks-old to be sung for in the marquee in the evening. A number of villagers competed, including Tustin Finch who sang, 'Tom Bowling'; Shepherd Chandler sang 'We are all jolly fellows who follow the plough'. The pig was won by Fanny Chandler. She seemed to have a way with pigs. The winner was the one who could sing without laughing and could keep the pig quiet. In her herden sacking apron in front of her cotton dress, Fanny never smiled, even when the pig relieved itself as she sang and soaked her clothes. She sang sweetly and with feeling.

> 'The tears rolled down her sunburnt cheeks
> and dropped on the letter in her hand.
> Is it true, too true
> More trouble in our native land.'

So with Scarrot's brightly painted ginny horses giving rides to the children, and the young and gallus riding high in the swinging boats, the end of Club Day drew near. As the Cheltenham supporters loaded up into the grand carriages which were to take them back twelve miles to town, the black horses with silver mounted harness, their manes and tails beribboned with blue, scraped the hard road with their hooves, impatient to get on their journey. Crowds of folk waved them off that evening.

Adam drove Noble in the dray with half the band back to Alderton. 'Where's Tustin?' Mr. Bushell said.

'Don't know sir,' Adam replied, and Jones drove Merriman in the dray with the rest of the band.

Late that night as Singer Sallis shut up his pub he heard singing from the stable. With a lantern he investigated, finding Tustin standing in the manger singing 'Dolly Gray'.

'Yes, my lad, Master Bushell ull want to know in the morning why you didn't drive the band home. He'll give you "Goodbye Dolly, I must leave you" tomorrow.'

Tustin weaved his way from the stable saying, 'It's only eleven months, two weeks and a fortnight to Ayshon Club.'

The year 1911 was surely a special year for the villages around Bredon Hill for soon after the Club Feast the Coronation celebrations were under way. The hill itself, that nine hundred foot mass of limestone covered by trees at the summit and oozing enough spring water to supply a large town, was the focus of the celebrations, and the great land owners who had their country houses on exactly opposite sides of the hill made the arrangements.

They were General Sir Francis Davies of Elmley Castle Park, one of a long line of distinguished soldiers, and Sir Richard Martin of Overbury Court, whose estate lay on the sunny south side of the hill and around the tower called Parson's Folly on Bredon summit. Fred Bushell from Ayshon Manor, like the other chief land owners of the hill villages co-operated with Sir Richard and the General in arranging the torchlight procession which turned out to be so illuminating.

The *Evesham Journal* reported it as follows:

Bredon Hill was the scene of one of the most interesting celebrations at night. The torchlight processions which started from various points and proceeded by appointed routes to the bonfire were seen from considerable distances and by a large gathering on the hill. The occasion was one that will not soon be forgotten. The torchlight procession assembled at nine o'clock. The villagers were allotted the following starting points. Those from Beckford, Overbury and Conderton assembled at the top of the new road; Kemerton at Barnes Buildings; Westmancote and Bredon's Norton at the bridle gate north west of the New Plantation; Eckington, Burlingham at the second gate above Wollas Hall on direct path to the Tower; Great Comberton, the footpath between Batten's Wood and the Camp; Little Comberton two hundred yards below Hopton's Gorse on a direct footpath; Elmley Castle and Ayshon the corner of the Long Plantation near Hopton's Gorse. All these places are within fifteen minutes of the Tower. The torches were served out at 9.15, lit at 9.30. At 9.35 the procession started as a signal rocket was fired from the Tower. At 9.50 they halted at arranged halting places and five minutes later on the firing of a single gun they moved to their appointed lines.

At ten o'clock a signal rocket was fired and 'God Save the King' and 'Rule Britannia' were sung. Roman candles were discharged and the Hill was illuminated by coloured fire.

'Oh God our help in ages past', 'Now thank we all our God', were also sung. The fireworks and bonfire followed.

What an evening that was on the Hill in that hot summer of 1911. Some said the few spots of rain which fell at tea time was the only rain that season. Sharp and short the storm was, just enough to make the dusty road smell sweet before the Ayshon men made their way to Hopton's Gorse for the procession.

'A tidy step to Parsons Folly for a man my age,' Bert Chandler complained to Mr. Bushell in the Manor sheep pens that morning as he marked a bunch of early fat lambs for Evesham Fair.

'That's arranged. Harry Carter's coming over from Donnybrook with his cob, Dick, and the governess cart. He's promised to take me up the hill to the Lodge Farm to my friend Mr. Meakins and stable there, and we will walk to Hopton's Gorse and then to the Tower. You can come along, Bert.'

'Capital,' Bert replied with a chuckle. 'I'd like to see the bonfire and see Joe Green again after many years, and I can walk on to Great Hill to see the sheep in the morning.'

Joe Green, who worked an allotment at Hill Withy alongside Durgin, was keeper of the Tower, known also as the summer house to the Hill people. He lived in a barn owned by the Martin family who had built him a fireplace and chimney and given him the office of looking after the squat building built by Squire Parsons about 1790 as a summer house. From here the view of the countryside was second to none. Cobbett said so in *Rural Rides*. The chequered counties of the Midlands and the middle west, the Severn Vale, the Malverns, the Welsh mountains, Clee Hill, Worcester cathedral, Gloucester cathedral, the Bristol Channel on clear days, and the nearby Cotswolds.

Joe was a recluse, a kind of hermit who charged tuppence per person if they wished to climb the spiral stone staircase to the top of Parsons Folly. His diet of fat bacon, rabbits, field mushrooms, potatoes, blackberries and vegetables in season made him perhaps the most self-sufficient man around Bredon. His barrel of cider was yearly taken with horse and cart to Joe Green's barn by the cider-makers of the Martin estate. No man who Bert Chandler or Fred Bushell knew was a match to Joe Green. He kept his pig in the barn adjoining his bothy. His geese grazed the trenched area of the old iron age camp, his fowls the Martin stubble. Joe studied the stars, the seasons, the trees. His uncanny knack with trap and snare was a secret he never divulged. He could imitate the call of hare or fox and bring them to his barn. It was known that Joe did snare a deer in season but how and when and where, no one knew. The hung buck in Joe's barn had been one reason why Bert Chandler paid him visits from the sheep barn at Great Hill. Bert would swop a home-made cheese for a haunch of venison, a couple of pounds of butter for a hare.

On Coronation night Bert decided to stay until morning with Joe. Fanny, Bert's wife, was not surprised. For years ago Bert had stayed at the barn overnight after a day in the sheep fold on Great Hill.

'This is the third caper that I've seen up here on the hill and no doubt you have too, Bert,' Joe said as they stood in the doorway and saw the flames from the fire shoot up above the battlements of the Tower.

'Ah, the Queen's two Jubilees you mean,' Bert replied.

The light of the fire, the rockets, illuminated La Loo farm half a mile away, tucked among the beech trees by the Dew Pond. It shone over Sleldon and Cobber's Quar. Both men thought deeply as they supped last year's cider. 'Remember the Russians with dancing bears staying at La Loo and the dancing bears at the Yew Tree pub?'

'Ah,' Bert replied. 'That did never interest me like the German bands who played on summer nights in Overbury Street. Uniforms were smart, ya know.'

Harry Carter looked over the Vale and saw the gas-lit town of Evesham six miles away. 'Come Michaelmas I'll be at the Lower Farm with you as landlord. I look forward to that,' he said to Fred Bushell.

'Soon pass, Harry, it'll soon pass, and you'll be here in time for the rabbiting.'

As they got into Harry's governess cart together the whole contingent of Ayshon men walked past on their way home; Durgin Green, Tustin Finch, Adam Hunt, Arthur Jackson, who walked with Ruby Bushell, Fred's son.

'Soon be the wedding,' Harry remarked.

'Ay, next month. I'll be glad to get Ruby settled and I believe Mildred's father thinks that about his daughter. You're not driving home tonight, Harry, you can stop at my place,' Fred suggested.

'It's all right, Mr. Bushell, I'm staying with Tom at Stanley Farm. I expect he's home by now, but he's courting a girl from Donnybrook. He'll come back from Evesham on his bike.'

So the celebrations ended at Ayshon.

Tom Bowman had spent the Coronation evening in the Donnybrook area of Evesham. He and his girl friend, Lily Westwood, walked late up Bridge Street to see the decorations and were surprised to find a crowd of six to eight hundred swarming the Market Place shouting and jeering.

Together Tom and Lily walked through the churchyard under the bell tower across the paddock and into the Crown yard where Tom had stabled his cob, Polly. As the two young folk hooked her between the shafts they heard the din from the Market Place and Merstow Green, louder and louder as the governess cart left the yard.

'Take me back to Port Street, Tom, then you had better make for Ayshon,' Lily said, holding tight to Tom's arm.

'Back early aren't you,' Mrs. Westwood said as she met them both at the door of number fifty.

'Trouble in the Market Square, so we came away,' was Tom's answer. 'I wonder what's gone wrong?'

Harry Carter laughed on Coronation night as Tom drove Polly into the yard of Stanley Farm. 'Had a good time in town, Tom?' he said. 'We've had a clinking time on the Bredon Hill.'

'There's something radically wrong in the town Harry tonight, there's an angry mob in the Market Place.'

Tom, Lily, Harry and the Ayshon folk had no idea how the celebrations had turned sour at Evesham until next day when Jack Gardener came over to the village to work. All Jack said was the trouble happened on account of a ball for the toffs. It wasn't until they received their copies of the *Journal* that the details of the whole sad affair came out. It appeared Evesham folk still nursed a grievance from 1901 and the postponing of Edward VII's Coronation, because of the King's illness, when a meal for all the townsfolk was not postponed, but cancelled. This time, for George V, the Town Council decided that the children only should have a party in the town. But a ball was arranged in the Public Hall for whoever pleased to dance the night away. Some rough characters who were customers at the Bewdley Street pubs said that the ball was being paid for out of the rates for what they called the toffs.

The Mayor, Mr. Hughes, known as Bodger, was a publican on Merstow Green. He was a benevolent man, always willing to help the poor and his contributions to charity at Christmas and at all times were unequalled in the town. Being Mayor he took the brunt of the Council's decision.

As the revellers went up the Public Hall steps they were hissed and booed at by a sprinkling of people in the square. 'Paid for by the rates!' some called. 'A disgrace to the town!' others chanted.

At ten o'clock two men in the square shouted loudly, 'Men of Evesham are you afraid? Who is going to fetch Bodger?'

At ten thirty a little man said, 'Bodger has got half an hour, then we go for him.'

Meanwhile one hundred and thirty Bewdley Street men were burning an effigy of Bodger Hughes outside his Merstow Green pub. One wonders whether the publicans were jealous of Bodger Hughes' pub on the Green and plied their customers with drink to cause trouble. That is exactly what happened. As the dance went on at the Public Hall the mob tried hard to enter the building. Outside, amid shouting, booing and dancing, the paper decorations were fired. The big archway in front of the Booth Hall was soon alight and the hall itself would have gone up in flames had it not been for the fire brigade.

As fireman Cook played his hose on the post office he was knocked out by the crowd and his hose pipe cut. The windows were broken in the Public Hall as the deputy Mayor attempted to speak to the mob. The police were outnumbered and reinforcements came by horse and carriage from Worcester. As the Superintendent told one Evesham man, 'You ought to be ashamed of yourself,' he had the reply, 'What's it to do with thee?'

In court the following week as the ringleaders stood in the dock, the Chairman of the Magistrates heard one of them testify that Cook the fireman played the hose on him.

'They don't seem to like cold water,' the Chairman commented.

A witness interrupted, 'We don't care for none of you, we have a right to speak as well as the toffs. We pay rates.'

Perhaps a tea for the children and a ball for those called toffs did leave a lot out in the cold as regards celebrating the Coronation of a monarch. At three o'clock the mob dispersed and only then was it safe for the ladies with sweeping dresses and the dapper young men of the town to leave the Public Hall.

7

Apple Christening Day

If on Swithin's Feast the welken lours
And every penthouse streams with hasty showers,
Twice twenty days shall clouds then fleeces drain
And wash the pavements with incessant rain.

John Gay

SAINT SWITHIN DIED IN THE YEAR 862 AND WAS BURIED according to his wishes outside the church at Winchester.

On 15th July 971, following his adoption as the patron of Winchester, the officials attempted to remove his remains to a better situation more fitting for a saint in a new basilica. The gentle spirit of St. Swithin objected and arranged for a downpour which lasted forty days. A country almanac of 1675 reads, 'If St. Swithin weeps the proverb says, the weather will be foul for forty days.'

In Somerset, Wiltshire and Ayshon's county of Gloucestershire, the day is known as Apple Christening Day. The old belief that it's wrong to gather apples before they have been christened by St. Swithin is very general and was observed by men like Fred Bushell, Bert Chandler and Durgin. The christening of apples is supposed to affect their flavour.

Saint Swithin's Day in 1911 passed with what Bert Chandler described as, 'Just a mizzle a bait time. Enough to christen the apples but no more.'

Young Adam Hunt picked a couple of Beauty of Bath apples as he passed through the Home Orchard on his way back from Didcot Ham where he and Noble had been drawing water with a muck cart and a hogshead cider barrel from Carrants Brook. The brook was running a small trickle of water. The springs on Bredon Hill were low and Adam stanked the brook by the red withies, bucketing

118

the water into the barrel for Mr. Bushell's cows grazing on the Ham.

The eels in the muddy bed of the stream wriggled their way into the pool which Adam created. Adam's mother and his father, John, were fond of the eels from Carrants Brook, so Adam caught a couple of the bigger ones and took them home for his mother to skin, to stew with parsley sauce for their supper.

As he came to the top of Gypsy's Lane, Bert Chandler was on his way home with his dog Rosie. Home from his sheep on the Hill. 'How many loads have you drawn today, my bwoy?' Bert Chandler asked young Adam.

'Four, Shepherd. I suppose your sheep have enough water still up on Paris Hill?' Adam replied.

The old man stood still in his tracks, leant on his crook and said, 'Adam my bwoy, ship beunt so thirsty as the milking cows. The early morning dew is almost enough for the yows, but they do drink in the heat of the day from the trough behind Paris Gardens. Cows be different though, and I do think that when water has to be drawn for them in such a summer as this, they drink for the sake of it.'

As Noble drew the cartload of water through the gate into the Ham, the cows left the loppings from the withy trees where Tustin had felled the leafy boughs for fodder during the day and ran towards the empty trough. Adam ran one hundred and twenty gallons of brook water into their trough then stood awhile watching the cows drinking.

Up at the White Hart, Singer Sallis stood behind his bar drawing beer from his cool cellar for Bert Chandler, Arthur Jackson and Tustin. 'How are Master Bushell's pheasant chicks, Arthur?' Singer enquired.

'They're coming along well in the coops in Straights Furlong, the best lot we have had for years. The drought suits 'em.' Singer who was one of the guns invited by Fred Bushell for the autumn shoots, looked forward to the October diversion from the pub, standing in the ride in Ayshon wood and bagging the birds.

'Oy, no doubt Arthur's learnt a wrinkle or two off his brother who's keeper up at Dumbleton,' Bert Chandler observed.

Arthur replied, ' 'Tis handy for me to rear the pheasants in the field by the wood. Fred Bushell pays me a bit of course, then I can take my place with my twelve bore when the beaters drive the birds on Saturdays in the autumn.'

Arthur had, it's true, learnt quite a bit about keepering from his brother. He fed the pheasant chicks in early summer from meal and corn but also from ant eggs. He could be seen on Cank's Bank, that tussocky elder-covered hillock, digging the ant hills with a spade then carrying a bucket of the white ant eggs to the young birds. A string line from Arthur's garden gate to a larch tree was loaded with predators; stoats, weasels, hawks, jays and magpies.

But Bert Chandler, whose heart and soul were in livestock,' turned the subject. 'You bin lopping withies today, Tustin, no doubt?' he ventured.

'Ah, it's a regular job finding a bite for the cows, something green, now the mangolds are over,' Tustin replied.

Tom then told his friends what a monotonous job young Adam had—'sading' he called it—drawing water and that he read in the *Journal* that in the next village a crop of oats had been cut with the binder and ricked in July when the seed was only planted in February.

'They never stopped in the stocks and heard the church bells ring for three Sundays before being carried, as is the custom,' Singer said.

'No,' Tom replied, 'the straw would be too parched to be any use for fodder with three weeks' sun on it, and mind you, every morsel of fodder will be wanted next winter. The hay smells sweet but 'tis a light crop this year and if the rain doesn't come there will be no lattermath to graze. Still, I'll be drawing the Lloyd George at Michaelmas and young Ruby ull be shepherd. 'Tis to be hoped that Mildred will make a man of him when they get married on Saturday. You be best man beunt ya, Arthur?'

Arthur nodded.

'Ruby's a fool to himself in company with the racing school in Cheltenham. Spirit drinking with that bag of sovereigns left him by his poor old mother. I often wonder what old Nehemiah, his gran-dad from Elmley, would have thought if he knew his hard-earned money was being used in that way.'

'Hard-earned?' Tustin interrupted. 'When Nehemiah rode with the Croome Hunt three times a week?'

'Now it don't become ya to speak like that of the dead. Nehemiah farmed when times were hard and lost a flock of ship with liver fluke in 1897.'

As they left the White Hart, Bert Chandler put his hand on Arthur's shoulder saying, 'Get young Ruby to church on Saturday in time for his wedding and get him there sober.'

On Saturday morning at the Manor Fred Bushell was up early. Arthur arrived at ten o'clock from Wood Farm to drive Fred Bushell's cob and trap to Cheltenham with the bridegroom. The wedding was to be at the parish church at half past twelve. Singer Sallis arrived with his mare and victoria promptly at ten and picked up Fred Bushell and Tom Bowman to drive to Ayshon station. Adam came along to drive Singer's outfit back to the White Hart when the ten twenty train arrived. Harry Carter joined them on the Evesham train, a smartly dressed Evesham man, a market gardener counting the days when he, with Tom, would rent Lower Farm from Mr. Bushell.

As the party changed trains at Ashchurch Junction Fred Bushell was looking worried. 'You'll be glad when today's over no doubt Mr. Bushell,' was Singer Sallis' comment.

'You know, Singer, Ruby's seldom sober and no doubt had a fair drop last night at the White Hart along with his cronies. I had a job to get him up and dressed today. I just hope Arthur can get him to the church on time.'

'Arthur will manage that, I assure you, sir,' Singer replied.

Now Mildred Churchway was the only daughter of William and Mary Churchway of Cheltenham. William was station master at Landsdown station. They had had their problems with their daughter, perhaps not in the same way as Fred Bushell had experienced with Ruby. Since leaving Pates Grammar school Mildred had been a nurse at the hospital. She was an auburn-haired attractive girl with a complexion like cream touched with roses. She had been courted by the engine drivers, firemen, signal men, guards — in fact most of the young men who worked around Cheltenham's Midland Railway Station.

Arthur Jackson and Ruby Bushell arrived at the Plough in Cheltenham at eleven o'clock. Arthur stabled the cob in the Plough yard. Ruby was impatient to have a livener in the hotel bar before facing the squad, as he called the invited guests, at the church. 'Take it steady Ruby, we must be in church by a quarter past twelve and you haven't recovered from last night's stag party yet.'

"I've a damn good mind not to go through with it, Arthur. It's a put up job between Father and William Churchway,' he replied.

'Your father has got the Middle Farm, a good house, buildings and orchard all ready for you and Mildred. And fancy waking up in the morning to find such a beauty as her beside you in the bed.'

Ruby's fuddled brain did register then at this prospect. As Ruby sipped his whisky, Arthur told him that he would not be many minutes away, but he had a gun in the trap to be repaired at Green's, the gunsmiths in the Strand. When Arthur returned he found Ruby a little unsteady with his arm round a buxom barmaid.

'This is my bride, Eva from Grove Street.' His hand slipped around her ample breast. 'Isn't she lovely, Arthur? Tell Mildred I'm not coming to church.'

'Don't be silly, darling,' Eva said with a laugh. 'You can see me any time after the honeymoon, when you are here with the boys.'

Arthur fetched Ruby's case from the trap and thought it to be on the light side. 'Are you packed ready for Bournemouth?' he said.

' 'Tis all in there that I want. You want to check it, Arthur?'

Arthur opened the case, amazed at what he saw. There were two Oxford shirts, a pair of braces, a broad leather belt and a pair of hob-nailed boots. Arthur held the boots by the laces. He and Eva laughed heartily. 'Are you expecting some heavy going at Bournemouth, Ruby? She's a woman of the world, you know.'

'Not the world, only the Midland Railway,' was the reply.

Ruby staggered to his feet like a cow recovering from milk fever. It put Arthur in mind of what Bert Chandler said about Stow Fair. A farmer took two horses there to sell, one to lean on the other to keep it up. He couldn't send one on its own. 'Come on, Ruby, time for church.'

The two men made their way down High Street into Clarence Street and through the churchyard. The first tombstone was in memory of a pig-killer named Higgs. Arthur did his best to put the fuddled bridegroom at his ease and read,

'In memory of Afred Higgs,
A famous man for killing pigs.
Now killing pigs was his delight
Both morning, afternoon and night.'

He then read one of a blacksmith 'whose fire was doubted, his anvil silent.'

'Where's the one, Arthur, about the woman who drank the Cheltenham waters?' Ruby asked as they stood together under the wall. Arthur recited,

'Here lie I and my three daughters
Who died from drinking the Cheltenham waters.
If we had have stuck to Epsom Salts
We wouldn't have been in these here vaults.'

'Cheltenham waters,' Ruby replied, 'Cheltenham ale. Hell's delight, the clock has just chimed a quarter past twelve.'

Both men sat in the front pew in the parish church. Mrs. Churchway, the bride's mother smiled at Arthur as she took her seat across the aisle. Behind the groom sat Fred Bushell with Reverend Edward Rushton, Vicar of Ayshon. In a seat towards the back of the church Singer Sallis sat with Harry and Alice Carter and Tom Bowman.

The bride arrived on her father's arm. She looked absolutely lovely. Her smiles for Ruby were apparently wasted. He would have been fast asleep but for the constant nudges of Arthur. 'A face like Mary Anderson the actress,' Tom Bowman whispered to Harry Carter.

Harry, a pretty good judge of the ladies, whispered back, 'She's a stunner.' Alice looked at him as a mother would look at a naughty boy.

The reception at the Plough Hotel was one with few speeches. Reverend Rushton proposing the toasts to the pair dwelt mainly on the qualities of Ruby's father whom he described as, 'that yeoman under Bredon, respected for his integrity for miles around'. He did say that Mildred looked angelic in her wedding gown, and was a tender nurse from the hospital, then he spoke of Ruby's superb horsemanship in the hunting field and at point to point. By now the groom was sobered up and, as Arthur said afterwards, he looked at the bride in a carnal fashion, picturing her in the bridal bed at Bournemouth with him in his Oxford shirt.

William Churchway had arranged for a car to take the couple to Malvern Road Station, a Great Western line for Bournemouth. He would have liked them to embark at Landsdown Midland where he was station master, but that was not to be.

Arthur Jackson had Singer Sallis in Fred Bushell's trap to accompany him home to Ayshon. They drove straight to the White Hart pub where Bert Chandler broke the news that Arthur's cattle had got out of the Wood Meadow and were in Frank Bishop's sainfoin field on the hill.

The field, known as the Leasow, was ready for mowing—Frank's last field for making hay. Arthur and Singer collected the dog from the woodhouse, rounded up the cattle and drove them to the meadow. During the few hours they had been in the sainfoin hay field they had trampled the ley flat around the headland and the news had reached Frank Bishop. He raced up the hill on his cob, meeting the men as they mended Arthur's fence.

'Gadding about at weddings, young fellow, and neglecting your fences. You'll pay for the damage!' he shouted as he saw the trampled ley.

'State your price, Mr. Bishop. I'll pay,' Arthur replied.

The following Thursday a general meeting was held in the school of Ayshon Cricket Club, chaired by the young curate, Mr. Hornsby. The secretary read a letter from Mr. Frank Bishop who as owner of the Broadenham field and President of the Club wrote saying that in future he refused to let one of the members, Arthur Jackson, play in any match during the season on his ground, owing to some grievance between themselves. The Chairman then explained that it was the duty of the members to consider the matter and decide if Mr. Jackson had broken any of the rules of the Club, and also to decide what steps should be taken in the matter.

Mr. Mitton, a newcomer to the village, proposed that it be put to the meeting whether Mr. Jackson be barred from playing in any other match during the season or not. This was seconded. The meeting, in the absence of Mr. Jackson, then on condition that Mr.

Jackson could not give a satisfactory explanation to prove he had not broken rule seven of the Club, divided on Mr. Milton's proposal.

For playing Mr. Jackson	5 votes
Against playing Mr. Jackson	12 votes
Majority against	7 votes

Mr. Bishop then agreed for the other matches to be played on his field and agreed to let the ground to the Club for another season at a yearly rent of one pound.

'How can rule seven have been broken?' Fred Bushell said, and read rule seven from the Minutes of the January meeting: ' "The Committee reserve the right to dismiss any members for disorderly or bad conduct on the ground." No such conduct is Arthur Jackson guilty of. The decision is a farce. I shall withdraw my support for the Club and hope that many more will follow.'

After that meeting, Fred Bushell, Arthur Jackson and Singer Sallis met at the Manor. The idea that for them village cricket had come to such an early end was unthinkable. 'I'll show Curate Hornsby and his Committee that we are not beholden to Bishop or his field. There are several flat fields on the Manor Farm,' Fred uttered in a voice choked with emotion. He added, 'Ruby will be back on Saturday and I'd like you and him to take the big roller down to the New Piece by the railway line and roll a strip of turf. I'll buy a practice net and we will start a team.'

'But, sir, we can't make a cricket field this dry summer, 'tis July, the ground's as hard as the devil's back teeth,' Singer Sallis remarked.

Fred Bushell then said that he would put an advert in the *Journal* asking for away matches only for the Ayshon United Cricket Club and that he would contact farmers in Evesham and Tewkesbury market and arrange fixtures. Next week, Singer Sallis, Arthur Jackson, Tustin Finch, Ruby, Adam Hunt, Jones and Tom Bowman, practised in the new net bought by Fred Bushell.

'We haven't got an eleven yet, sir,' Adam said to his master.

'Never mind, Adam. Arthur Jackson is getting some players from Hinton and Sedgeberrow.'

The first match for the United Club was fixed for August Monday at Littleton and Fred Bushell promised that he would get the New

Piece ready for home matches for next year. He gave twenty pounds as his donation for the fund. Arthur Jackson gave five pounds, Singer Sallis five pounds, Harry Carter two pounds, Tom Bowman two pounds and Ruby Bushell gave two pounds; making thirty-six pounds in all. Singer Sallis was appointed Treasurer, Ruby Bushell was appointed Secretary and Arthur Jackson, Captain.

When Reverend Rushton heard of the United Club he drove over to the Manor to see Fred. 'I'm in a very difficult position, Fred,' he said. 'You see my curate, Hornsby, has made what I call a dubious decision. I must support him in the church, but I'll endeavour to be neutral and support both our teams.'

Fred Bushell eyed the parson, puffed his pipe and said, 'People who live in glass houses should not throw stones, but I carry a stone a long while before I eventually throw it.'

Reverend Rushton smiled, changing the subject. He told Fred that the Ayshon Club would miss Arthur, their best bowler. 'How about the kit for your club, Fred? Bats, wickets and such like?'

'Singer has been to Woop's of Cheltenham and spent twelve pounds on the gear,' Fred replied.

As the hot days of July became shorter, Arthur Jackson's pheasant chicks wandered away from the coops to Ayshon wood. Here Arthur kept a watchful eye for the predators. Fred Bushell sent Ruby with a horse and float up the Seeds, through the ten acre piece to Staights Furlong where the birds were. He took with him more corn from the rickyard and a rearing mixture from West Midland Farmers Association. 'Shall we have a good show of birds for the October shoot, Arthur?' young Ruby enquired.

'Pretty good, but there's no money for your Dad in this venture. 'Tisn't exactly farming, Ruby. The old saying is with pheasants at a shoot, up goes seven shillings and six pence (the cost of rearing a bird), bang goes two pence (the cost of a cartridge), down comes half a crown (the worth of a shot pheasant). Mind, Ruby, I bought the broody hens cheap at three shillings a piece and they will be worth perhaps four shillings a piece when they start laying after the chicks have been taken from them.'

Fanny Chandler arrived at the Manor early on a July Sunday morning. 'Our Bert's abed, Master, with water trouble. Doctor

Overthrow came here turned midnight and bought him some jallop but he's not able to work and he's worried about the ship on the hill,' she said.

Fred Bushell asked her to go and see Tustin and tell him to come to the Manor. 'I'll be along and see Bert this afternoon and tell him not to worry,' he said to the shepherd's wife.

'Do ya want me a-shepherding this morning, Gaffer?' were Tustin's words as he met Mr. Bushell at the dairy door.

'Ah, Bert's bad, Tustin, and we'll have to pen the ewes on Paris Hill and look them over for maggots. You go and fetch young Adam because Bert's dog, Rosie, will not work with us and we need another hand to pen the ewes in the Paris Slinget.'

Mr. Bushell, Tustin and Adam walked together up through Church Close, past the moat pond to the hill. The sun shone as bright and clear as ever as they passed the work horses lazing away the Sunday morning under the elder bushes, their long tails switching at the flies which tormented man and beast. 'What's the horse whip for, Adam?' Fred asked the boy.

'You see, we ain't got a ship dog and I thought if I cracked the whip the yows would huddle together like and twould save us running about.'

'Good reasoning, boy, and you, Tustin, have you some maggot water in the frail basket and some Stockholm tar?'

'Yes, Master,' the young cowman replied.

Fred Bushell knew that the best time to check sheep for the fly was very early morning. Bert always looked them over at five o'clock.

The one hundred and fifty ewes were lying together under the two big oak trees over towards the cuckoo pen. With them were just twenty-five lambs, the remainder of two hundred odd which had been born the February before. The other lambs had been sold fat at Evesham and Tewkesbury markets.

'Now spread out, you young fellas. Adam, you follow the hedge by Quar Hill and you walk alongside the wall next the cuckoo pen, and I'll go around by the barn, then the stragglers will run to the shade of the oaks.' A few ewes did scamper to the shade from the thistles, near Quar Hill, then all three 'shepherds' closed in towards the oaks.

'Ho, ho, ho,' Tustin called, then the ewes moved a few at a time towards Paris. Fred Bushell whistled as if calling a dog but the ewes doubled back towards the shade. Adam cracked his ploughman's whip, scattering the sheep until they took a line following the shade of the hedge to the pen.

'Who gave you the idea of bringing a whip to drive the sheep, Adam?' Mr. Bushell asked.

'Father, sir, when he hurdled some lambs on the turnips on the hill years ago,' Adam replied.

Fred closed the hurdle of the pen in Paris Slinget and walked quietly among the flock. 'Catch that one, Tustin,' he called. Tustin crooked a ewe and brought it to his master.

The ewe was switching her short tail and looking around at her rump. Fred Bushell parted the wool on her fleece, exposing a bunch of maggots working in the soiled wool. 'Jeyes fluid,' he called.

Adam handed the bottle of maggot water. 'Pour a little just there,' he ordered Adam.

With a pair of shears Fred clipped the soiled wool from the sheep's breach, waited a minute for the fluid to kill the grubs, then he took a penny from his pocket and with it he scraped the dead maggots to the ground. The bare skin was punctured and inflamed, about the size of a walnut, so Fred called again, 'Stockholm tar from the frail, Adam.' The boy handed a jar of the black ointment which Fred applied to the wound. 'They heal very quickly,' he told his workers. 'But we will dip them on Monday and protect them from the bluebottle fly,' he added.

Standing in the corner near the water trough was a lamb Fred described as 'unkind'. 'Catch it Tustin,' he called. Tustin carried the lamb to Fred who clipped some soiled wool from its hindquarters. 'There—you see they have just started to strike. You see the yellow fly blows and a little bunch has just hatched into maggots.'

Fred applied the lotion, the maggots fell to the ground, the lamb was released. 'My boys,' Fred said to his workers, 'that lamb has doubtless got worms, it's not thriving, it scours, a sign of worms, always look for a sheep that appears uncomfortable.'

The rest of the flock were free of the fly. Fred opened the hurdle a little and told Tustin and Adam to drive them past him slowly to enable him to count them. 'You count the lambs, Adam, as they run through the gap and I'll count the ewes.'

As every ewe passed the farmer he touched it on its back with his stick, while Adam touched the lambs. 'Twenty-five lambs sir,' Adam spoke up as the last of the sheep left the pen. 'One ewe missing, there's only one hundred and forty-nine,' Fred said with a sigh. 'Reminds me of Durgin's hymn he was singing when he hoed Tom and Harry's sprouts. "There were ninety and nine that safely lay In the shelter of the fold, But one was out on the hills away, Away from the gates of gold." '

'Who wrote that?' Tustin said with his kind of sarcastic laugh.

'Moody and Sankey, the American evangelists,' Fred replied.

'Trust old Durgin to sing such a verse,' Tustin said.

'The fact is we have got to find that ewe for she could soon be eaten with maggots, Sunday or not,' were Fred Bushell's orders. 'You walk round the hedge alongside Church Close, Tustin. I'll follow the hawthorn bushes alongside Quar Hill, and you take the cart track alongside Clark's Orchard, Adam. We'll all three meet at the barn, one of us will surely find her.'

Clark's Orchard lay behind the thatched cottage known as Camp House, a cottage where it was said Oliver Cromwell tied his horse to an iron ring on one of the outside beams. It was occupied by Ern Meadows, a rabbit catcher. He kept a few geese and guinea fowls in the orchard.

Many's the time when Bushell's men came home at dusk from the hill when the guinea fowls, or glearies as they were called, could be heard with their distinct cry, 'Come back, Come back', as they roosted in the apple trees.

Fred drew a blank near Quar Hill, Tustin found nothing alongside Church Close, Adam walked closely to the orchard fence, if fence it could be called, for Ern failed to keep a good mound alongside this orchard. On two strands of barbed wire Adam noticed some fresh sheep's wool stained with blood. He looked across the orchard but the nettles grew high under the trees and he could see nothing. At the barn he told Mr. Bushell what he had seen. 'No doubt she's among the nettles. Bring the frail, Tustin, We'll go and see.'

Over the stile by the badger's earth they followed Mr. Bushell. As the ewe came from the cool of a patch of nettles Tustin grabbed her and pulled her to the ground. The soiled fleece, the smell of putrid flesh told one tale. She was struck badly by the fly. Fred Bushell clipped away a patch of wool near her hip bone and exposed a seething mass of wriggling grubs. 'Oh dear,' he said sadly. 'Bring the maggot water, Tustin.'

He poured half a bottle of Jeyes fluid in a deep hole which the maggots had eaten in her side. 'If it wasn't so serious sir, we could have a day's fishing with that lot. There must be a quart of the greedy sods.'

'Ah Tustin, Isaac Walton called them gentiles in his book. But let's get her in the shade. Fetch the stable wheelbarrow, Adam.'

When Adam arrived with the barrow and a little straw and a G.O. line, they lifted the ewe into it and roped her down with the G.O. rein. Tustin wheeled her to the half-lidded place next the bull pen while Fred sent Adam to Bert Chandler with a message asking Tom how to treat a ewe in such a condition.

'Tell Master Bushell to fill the cavity with dry wood ashes and she'll be as right as ninepence in a wick. Before you go,' Tom said, 'would you mind picking me some agrimony blossoms off the hill so that Fanny can make me some herb tea for my water. 'Twill do me more good than the doctor's jallop. Always did before. Can you get some after dinner?'

Adam agreed and went and told Mr. Bushell what Bert had suggested.

Oh, the ewe was soon better in the cool of the building and Bert's water was working again thanks to Adam's agrimony.

As July 1911 came to a close Tom Bowman and Harry Carter had Alf Miller and Jack Gardener picking the Prolific plums in Carrants Field. It's true the sample was small and had to be picked before they were quite ripe or else they cooked like prunes on the trees. Durgin drove Harry's light dray to market with the Telegraph peas. The pickers slept the nights and weekends away in the Cross Barn.

A motley crowd they were, taking a holiday in the sun from the streets of Birmingham and the Black Country. Every night Durgin weighed up the bags of peas on the tripod scales in the field. He gave the pickers cheques, metal discs with H.C. stamped on. Just another import to Ayshon Harry Carter brought with him.

He didn't like the idea of Durgin being loaded with money to pay the pickers in the evening, so they changed their cheques at Tom

Bowman's window when they needed money. Money for food, money for drink at the White Hart pub.

Tom Bowman read in the *Journal* of orchards of fruit for sale at Charlbury in Oxfordshire. Harry Carter was keen to buy, he had experience of buying fruit on the trees around Evesham. He, Tom, Jack and Alf were experts with the long ladders, while Durgin could weigh and pack, haul to market or station. 'I'll meet you, Tom, at Evesham Station on the morning of the sale. You'll be coming on the Midland from Ayshon?'

These words of Harry's were the final arrangement for fruit buying at Charlbury. They boarded the G.W.R. London train and rode to Charlbury Station. Here they made for the small hotel in the village and the auction. It appeared that men of Oxfordshire were not such gamblers as to buy apples in July when anything may happen. Harry and Tom were prepared to take that risk and bought two large orchards of Blenheim and souring apples.

'Busy you'll be in the autumn, Harry, fruit picking and moving to the Lower Farm, ay,' Fred Bushell said to this young Evesham grower.

'Them as lives longest ull see the most,' little Durgin said to Alf and Jack. 'But Harry and Tom be taking a risk. What a month it's bin,' he added, 'wedding, cricket and Bert Chandler taken abed.'

'Ay, and thee singing about the lost ship among Bowman and Carter's sprouts,' Tustin replied.

'Who was it milked the dry cow?' Durgin taunted.

Tomorrow would be August and the cricket match on Monday.

8

Lammas Day

AUGUST 1ST, LAMMAS DAY, THE FEAST OF THE FIRST FRUITS of harvest, was observed as an expression of gratitude to God for the crops. Lammas is derived from the Anglo-Saxon word *Hlafmaesse* or Loaf Mass, a day when the first wheat was cut, thrashed and made into bread, then offered in the churches. The modern Harvest Thanksgiving began with a service of gratitude by the Rev. R. S. Hawker, vicar of Morwenstow in Cornwall, in 1843. This was rather different from Lammas because Hawker's thanksgiving was held at the end of the harvest when all the crops were gathered in.

Lammas has had an important place in the farming calendar, and was once a rent day for the Lammas lands. These lands were let by the Manor for grazing or hay from Lady Day until August 1st, and from then on were common land grazed with the common by the strip holders with grazing rights. On Fred Bushell's Manor Farm a field next the church was known as Lammas Hey where the practice of a four-months let had been a recognised thing before the En-closures of Ayshon in 1783. The land stretched from the churchyard to the White Hart Inn. It's a well known fact that the church often stands on some of the best land in the parish. This certainly applied to Ayshon.

Fred recognised this when he planted Lammas Hey with fruit trees. It was here that he grew Warner King apples to perfection. The trees grew with straight branches as high as the White Hart. The Evesham merchants were eager to buy these cookers after Fred had stored them in the old Cross Barn until Christmas. Then the fruit was mellow. Beside them a row of Count von Bismark gave a splash of colour in Fred's orchard. But the main part of Lammas Hey had been planted with cider fruit. Black Tauntons, Fox Whelps, Golden Pippins, Redstreaks, the Royal Wilding and Pearmains. It was from here in Autumn when the fruit was ready that Bert Chandler took it to the cider mill near the duck pond at the Manor and milled and pressed the fruit for the men's cider.

Fred used to like to entertain his friends and offer them Perry from the pears in Lammas Hey, the Huffcaps, Oldfields, Barlands, Malvern Hills, Chisel Pears and the Black Pear of Worcester.

There was one thing that Mr. Bushell and Reverend Rushton agreed upon – the Harvest Festival at the end of the harvest, which had overshadowed Lammas.

'It's not according to the Bible, Fred,' the parson said. 'But I take your point it's so much better to give thanks when your ricks are built and your barns are full. So much can happen to the corn after Lammas.'

'Many a slip twixt the cup and the lip,' Fred quoted. He smiled and thought of Jim Cambridge that Birmingham iron master who was more impatient than the dyed-in-the-wool yeoman of Ayshon. 'Jim does count his chickens before they are hatched,' he said to the parson. 'I've seen him,' he added, 'with his note book estimating how many sacks of wheat will be harvested off the Ten Acre Piece. Then comes the wind, the tempest, the hail stones, flattening the crop. The binder will not cut the lain corn so it's a job for the men sweating with hook and crook as they did in Grandfather's time.'

After the tropical heat of the summer of 1911, harvest was over by August bank holiday. the crops were light, but the grain was dry, only the beans were still in stook.

After the bank holiday Monday when many of the Ayshon folk had spent the day at Bricklehampton Flower Show, after walking five miles round Bredon Hill to the field near the Hall, Fred Bushell went again to his bean field in Ramacre. He picked up a sheaf and in doing so the horse beans rattled from their pods on to the black stubble known as bean brisk. He looked up at the blue sky where the sun poured out its blistering heat and he wondered – he had a good crop here on the heavy clay near the railway line. The land had been dressed with the previous year's cattle yard muck, before it had been ploughed by Adam and Jones.

Early next morning he left the Manor before breakfast. The heavy morning dew soaked his boots as he walked down Cinder Meadow.

In the bean field he found the bean pods and the straw quite wet with dew; picking up a sheaf he threw it to the ground as hard as a sheaf would fall on a waggon. The dew-soaked pods hardly shed any of their corn. He said to himself, 'Ah, it looks like we'll have to carry them at night, when dew is on the stooks.'

Back in the stable, Adam was bringing in the horses from the field in readiness for the mowing on the Hill. 'Tie them up Adam, then help the shepherd with the sheep. When you have finished get off back to bed.'

Adam's mouth was wide open, 'Do you mean that, sir?' he muttered.

'We are carrying the beans after sunset, Adam, to prevent them shedding.'

As Tustin and Jones came to the yard Fred told them the same story. It was agreed to work all night.

'Do you want me to take part in this caper? 'Cos I a done it years ago, but can't remember how long,' Bert Chandler asked his master.

'I'd be glad if you would build the rick. It's moonlight tonight, Bert, I believe.'

'Comes up over Broddy monument as big as a waggon wheel he do, and you can almost see to read the *Journal*,' Bert replied.

Fred Bushell rode his cob up to the Wood Farm and saw Arthur Jackson. He told Arthur what he intended to do, so Arthur promised to come and help haul the beans. 'We really want to work double-handed you know, Mr. Bushell,' Arthur suggested.

'I know what you mean, Arthur, some pitching, others unloading.'

'Why not ask Tom and Harry to help, I'm sure they would,' Arthur said.

'I'm popping into Evesham this morning and I'll see Harry in the Smithfield Market.' Fred drove to town and enlisted Harry Carter. He met Tom Bowman as he came away from his pea fields – Tom promised to help, so all was set for the moonlight harvesting.

Fred and his son, Ruby, took a horse and dray with a load of straw and made a staddle for the bean rick in Ramacre. 'I'll bring Durgin along with me,' Tom Bowman said to Mr. Bushell. 'He's a good loader on the waggon.'

At nine o'clock that evening Adam Hunt led Noble and Merriman down to the bean field, pulling one of Fred Bushell's waggons. Jones followed with Pleasant in the shafts of another waggon. The men met at nine thirty and the evening light was soon replaced by what Bert Chandler called 'The parish lantern.'

'Will you and Tom pitch?' Fred said to Harry Carter.

'If we can't we'll make it as nobody else can,' Harry replied with a laugh and grabbed a shuppich or pitchfork.

'You load, Durgin, with Tustin,' were Fred's orders.

At the rick to help Bert Chandler the rick-builder, were Ruby, Jones and Arthur Jackson. Adam drove the horses to and from the stooks to the rick. 'Do you think we'll be put in the Cheil, sir?' Tustin said with a grin. The Cheil was a column in the *Evesham Standard* reporting something out of the ordinary in the Vale; a sort of skit on people; like when the Yubberton folk lifted the pig on the wall to hear the brass band go by.

'Did they put thee in there when you milked that dry cow?' Durgin interrupted. 'Up in this waggon alongside me, thee hast too much of what the cat licks himself with. I'll load the front end and you the back, we'll load boat-fashion,' he added.

Now, boat-fashion made it a little easier for the pitchers. It was a way of loading a waggon keeping the load low in the middle until the load was on. The pitchers tossed their sheaves to the low part of the load.

'Hold tight,' Adam called as the horses pulled the waggon between the rows of stooks.

'Mind and remember to call every time, "Hold tight." You'll have us ass over head off the waggon else,' Durgin said to the boy.

Tom and Henry soon had a load of beans on the waggon. Arthur Jackson pitched the sheaves off the load to Ruby who tossed them to Jones, while Bert Chandler stacked them in neat rows on the rick.

At midnight under the moon Fred Bushell came through the gate to the field with a horse and float. 'I've brought you an urn of tea. Sit down for a few minutes and slake your thirst.'

'No cider then, Gaffer?' Tustin called from the load.

'No, not tonight. You need a clear head on the waggon or on the rick working in the shadows,' he replied.

Durgin drank tea from the crock tot, turned to Tustin saying, 'Can't you leave the cider alone just for one night? Anyone would think you were weaned on it.'

'So I was, that and a nice young woman. Takes some beating,' Tustin replied. Durgin bit his lip, said nothing and looked at Fred Bushell who gave him a knowing smile.

By half past four half the field had been carried and ricked so the men made their way home. 'After the sheep and cattle have been attended to get some rest ready for tonight,' Fred told his men.

Harry Carter went with Tom Bowman to Stanley Farm, then after breakfast they went to the pea field. At mid-day Tom went to bed but Harry, who used to say he could sleep anywhere, just dossed down on the sofa.

Next day in Ayshon village street Fred Bushell met Reverend Rushton. 'Your men were working late last night, Fred. I heard noise of men, horses and waggons from the vicarage window at midnight.'

Fred Bushell replied, 'We worked all night, Parson, to save the beans. Had we carried them during the day half the corn would have scattered out in the sun. Now on Sunday you can sing, "All is safely gathered in".'

'Are you working tonight, Fred?'

'Yes, we'll about finish by three o'clock tomorrow morning.'

The vicar was a man who had quite immersed himself in the ways of the farming folk. He cultivated a large garden growing vegetables and flowers, the best of which were taken to the Harvest Festival at St. Barbara's. Labourers used to ask his advice on which variety of potatoes to plant, which breed of fowls laid the most eggs.

He kept Old English game poultry for the table. These broad-breasted fowl were moderate layers but the villagers bought the sitting eggs from the parson to place under their broody hens and produce chickens for Christmas poultry.

The vicar had been reared on his father's farm near Bridgnorth in Shropshire where, as a lad, he pitched and loaded the waggons, ploughed the land, planted the crops. His father was one of the old time squarsons (a parson squire). He, being the youngest son was sent to Cambridge and took Holy Orders. At Cambridge he won his boxing blue which stood him in good stead when he dealt with any form of violence among his flock. The fact that he had defended himself on that dark night in Rabbit Lane when a vagrant attempted to steal the church collection as the parson was on his way home from church, was never forgotten.

'I'll be along this evening and give you a hand, Fred,' the vicar suggested.

'Very welcome, Vicar, I know you are used to harvesting,' was Fred's reply.

'About nine o'clock I'll be in Ramacre with my own pitchfork. I'll enjoy that in the cool of the evening and night.'

The waggons and horses were taken to the field as before by Adam and Jones. The vicar was waiting in the field when the men arrived. He stood there in his shirt sleeves, collarless and wearing a Panama hat.

Tustin turned to Durgin as they passed through the gateway with these words, 'Hell's bells, if it yunt the Sky Pilot with a shepherd.'

'Now if he's come to lend a hand, as I'll warrant he has, just moderate your language, Tustin,' Durgin said.

'If he's a gwain to pitch we'll have to watch our legs when he uses that fork. I unt going to work along of a novice.'

Fred Bushell heard Tustin utter the last remark. He walked close up to him and said, 'Look here, Tustin, the Reverend pitched corn before your ass was as big as a sixpence. I don't want to hear any more of that talk.' Then he turned to the vicar. 'If you help Tom and Harry to pitch the sheaves that be setting as forward, Parson. I'm afraid you'll have to move from one row of stooks to the other, helping Tom and Harry as you see fit.'

'Fine, Fred,' the parson replied.

As Adam shouted, 'Hold tight,' from stook to stook the sheaves were tossed up to Tustin and Durgin. As the rick got higher in the corner of the field, Arthur was so busy unloading that no sooner had he emptied a waggon, Adam was there with another load. By half past one Arthur had difficulty in throwing the sheaves to the roof of the rick. 'We can do with an extra here, Master Bushell,' he called to Fred.

'Will you help, Vicar?' Fred asked the Ayshon parson.

'You need a harrow on the side of the roof instead of a pitch hole, I gather,' Reverend Rushton answered.

Fred nodded but was loth to ask the parson to stand on a harrow on the roof of the rick and take the sheaves off Arthur's fork, then pitch them to Jones and Ruby. Ruby found a harrow in the hedge from a set of three under the elms. He climbed the ladder, stuck the tines of the harrow firmly on the side of the roof of the bean rick and said, 'I'll stand on there, sir. It's a bit tricky, you know.'

Reverend Rushton climbed the ladder, smiled at Ruby, stood with the heels of his boots dug into the rickside and the insteps on the harrow. 'Let's have them, Arthur,' he said.

What a man to have in the harvest field. For he pitched to the left or to the right, taking the sheaves off Arthur's fork in a most professional way. Fred Bushell as he brought the urn of tea remarked, 'You know, sir, I'd pay you a bit more than the fifteen bob a week the men get if you'd like a job on the farm.'

Reverend Rushton answered, 'I'll tell you what, Fred, you take my job as parson and I'll do the farming.'

Bert Chandler who had had a bit of backchat with the vicar thought, ah, he did say he had got a flock to shepherd, and I told him how often my sheep had to be maggoted. He said nothing, but was impressed by the way the parson set about work.

As the men drank the tea and ate the bread and boiled bacon from Fred's float, Ruby walked under the elms and fetched a little barrel of cider; a four and a half gallon known as a pin. He lifted it on to a log of wood, turned the tap and drew a quart into a jug. He poured a tot for Tustin, one for himself and one for Arthur. 'Careful Ruby, we don't want any accidents you know, the cider's strong and we must keep our heads clear,' Fred cautioned.

'Try a tot, Vicar?' Ruby said.

The parson accepted and took a drink of what Bert Chandler called agricultural brandy. 'Yunt I having one then, Ruby?' Bert Chandler called from the rick, where he had his bacon and bread. Ruby climbed the ladder with a tot for the rick-builders. In a few minutes the empty waggon was between the last rows of stooked beans. Tom and Harry were pitching the sheaves once more. It was the last load.

When the ridge had been built on the rick, Fred Bushell pitched a few boltens of straw to Arthur's empty waggon. Arthur passed the straw to the parson while Bert Chandler built the bolting as a ridge to finish the stack.

'We had better empty that little barrel,' Ruby said to his father. Fred Bushell gave Adam a tot of cider and told him to take the horses back to the stable. The other men sat down under the rick. Harry, Tom Bowman, Fred and Durgin drank the tea from the urn, while Tustin, Ruby, Arthur, Bert Chandler and Jones all took deep draughts of the amber cider.

The vicar put on his coat and collar and once more became the parson of Ayshon. As the morning light came over the Cotswold Edge, Ruby and Tustin began to sing.

'All is safely gathered in, free from sorrow, free from sin,' sang Tustin.

The vicar found it a good opportunity to ask the men to attend the Harvest Festival on Sunday. 'Tustin, I'd be awfully glad to see you at Church on Sunday at the Harvest Festival. It's sad, you know, that you are one of the most regular bell ringers at St. Barbara's yet you seldom attend worship. I'd like to see you and the other ringers there more often.'

Tustin's turn of phrase didn't forsake him despite the effect of the cider. Durgin looked at him, almost through him, with that look which meant, now give an answer to that one, boy. 'Your Reverence,' Tustin began, 'we as rings the bells ud very very much like to see you up in the tower among the ropes sometimes.'

'He's got a point there you know, Vicar,' Fred Bushell remarked.

'I'll be in the tower Sunday morning. Now that's a bargain, Tustin, and you'll be at the service.'

Tustin grinned, showed his gappy teeth, took a swig of his cider and replied, 'You can ring the Tenor, that ull warm your shirt. Oh ah, I'll be along at the service.'

The harvest of 1911 was ricked and the men who had sweated through that blistering summer would be ploughing the stubbles as soon as the rain came to soften the top soil. 'I'll see to the cattle and sheep tomorrow, and you men can lie in,' Fred Bushell told them. 'Good morning to you all, my breakfast will be ready.'

'Thank you sir,' Bert Chandler replied.

Fred stepped into the float and his cob took him through the gate into Cinder Meadow and home, together with Tom Bowman and Harry. In the half light of morning, Tustin and Ruby danced around the bean rick, much to the disgust of Durgin.

'You chaps unt fitting to be along with decent men, shouting and hollering like as if you had a tile loose. Ought to be on some theatre stage I reckon. What do you think, Vicar?'

Durgin's words were weighed for a second or two before Reverend Rushton replied, 'Oh, I don't know Durgin. David danced before Saul when Saul was in a mood of depression, so it says in the Book.'

'I don't hold with dancing nor drink, it makes a fool of a man.'

'Oh, I've every respect for your ideas you Chapel folk, but it's a legacy you have from the old Queen's day. You make great emphasis on the word.'

' "Wine is a mocker, strong drink is raging, and whosoever is deceived thereby is not wise." '

'Paul says, when you are old "Drink no longer water, but use a little wine for thy stomach's sake." '

'The vicar knows his Bible I'll allow, but I believe in moderation in all things,' was Bert Chandler's comment.

Round the rick came Ruby and Tustin dancing and singing, while Bert, Arthur and Jones supped deeply at the cider. As Durgin sat on a bolting of straw finishing up the bread and boiled bacon, drinking tea from his enamel cup, Ruby and Tustin stopped in front of the little man. 'Now Durgin, I know thee canst sing, give us a verse or two of "There were ninety and nine", the one you sang up on Bredon among the sprouts.'

'That's one of Moody and Sankey's isn't it, Durgin?' was the vicar's question.

'Yes, and I can sing without having a gutsful of cider. I'll sing for you, sir.' Durgin stood up knowing he had an understanding ally in the parson, and sang, ' "Tell me the old, old story of Jesus and his Love." '

The vicar walked towards Durgin who was now standing in front of Ruby and Tustin; he held Durgin's hand saying, 'Now you know if you sing like that, it does more good than all the argument about your God and my God to break the ice for the critical folk in this world like Tustin.'

'I'll sing to you now,' Tustin ventured. 'Now Ruby, you join in with "Buttercup Joe".' He began, ' "I can drive a plough and milk a cow, and I can reap or mow." '

'I'm gwain home. How about you, Arthur?' Bert Chandler said.

'When we have sung, "We plough the fields and scatter the good seed on the land",' Arthur replied.

The vicar struck the first note as the men stood in a half circle round the rick and with feeling they sang,

> 'He sends the snow in winter,
> The warmth to swell the grain,
> The breezes and sunshine,
> The soft refreshing rain.'

Bert Chandler's sweet boyhood soprano had once rung like a bell in the chancel of St. Barbara's, bringing tears to the eyes of the old ladies of Ayshon. His singing now was just a memory among the oldest inhabitants after a lifetime among his sheep. He called out, 'Can we sing "Come ye thankful people come", before Arthur and I go home?'

The vicar, Tustin, Durgin, Ruby, Arthur, all agreed and with great feeling the words floated over the morning air in Ramacre field.

> 'All is safely gathered in,
> Ere the winter's storms begin.'

'We'll be along a Sunday, sir,' Bert promised. 'I'll meet ya by the lych gate at quarter past six, Tustin,' he added.

The Harvest Festival service was, as usual, well attended. Fred Bushell and Ruby and Mildred sat in a pew almost under what Bert Chandler called the Bird, that eagle lectern where the lesson was read by Doctor Overthrow.

Frank Bishop and his wife sat in the pew next to the middle aisle. Frank was not a favourite in the village, especially after the trouble with Arthur Jackson. In a short pew behind the organ were Arthur Jackson, Tom Bowman, Harry Carter and Alice. Harry and Alice were staying the weekend at Stanley Farm prior to them coming to live at the Lower Farm. Behind the font near the vestry door, sitting together in one pew, were Tustin Finch and the other ringers. In front of them sat Singer Sallis, Bert Chandler and Fanny.

A minute before the first hymn, a little figure came through the Norman porch, pushed aside the already drawn draught curtains and took a place beside Bert Chandler. It was Durgin Green. He brushed his greying hair aside as he walked carrying his Bible; at the pew he whispered to himself these words with bowed head, 'We enter, Lord, Thy Holy shrine, The place where Thou dost dwell. Oh hush each thought which is not thine And make us serve Thee well. Amen.'

The fruit and vegetables, despite the drought, were as good as usual. Singer Sallis' pumpkin, polished as a mammoth orange, took pride of place in front of the chancel steps. Durgin admired the flowers and the sheaves of wheat. 'Beunt no beans here, Bert,' he said.

'No, 'twood a made a mess, pods a shedding in the church,' he was answered.

Fred Bishop and Doctor Overthrow took up the collection. They walked smartly from the vestry door to the parson with their bags of money as he stood in front of the altar. Reverend Rushton's sermon was to the point. He stressed the importance of such a thanksgiving. He spoke of the gathering of the beans through the night with Mr. Bushell's men and was pleased to have taken a part in the ingathering.

Durgin Green walked down the path to the churchyard gates with Bert Chandler. 'Very good service, Bert,' he remarked. 'Not a lot of bowing and scraping. I don't hold with that, ya know.'

Bert Chandler stood under the beech tree with Durgin and lit his pipe. They listened to the five bells ringing, Bert remarking that they were round ringing, and that the tenor was being rung by Tustin.

'Glad to see him in the church, I was,' Durgin remarked. 'He says he's an unbeliever, ya know,' he added.

'Take that with a pinch of salt, Durgin. He says that just to rile you,' the shepherd answered.

'Are you having a Harvest Home this year, Bert?' Durgin said with interest, giving Bert the impression that he would like to come.

'Oh, yes, but 'twill be in September. Allus have been. You'll come of course 'cos you helped to carry the beans. I daresay Tom Bowman and Harry will be there, so you won't be the only teetotal.'

With these words Bert and Durgin parted, Bert going up the road to his cot by the White Hart and Durgin to his thatched black and white cottage under the walnut tree.

9

Michaelmas Goose

BY SEPTEMBER THE SPROUTS ON FRED BUSHELL'S HILL WERE
two foot six high while on every stem the buttons of green were
ready for picking off the bottom of the stems. Bowman and Carter
had bought two tons of nitrate of lime off Mr. Phipps of Evesham to
sow between the rows as a final tonic for the crop. This fertiliser, a
product of Norway, had the effect of providing both moisture and
feed to the roots of plants. Harry Carter scratched the soil away from
the plants as he showed Alf Miller how the small fibrous roots had
travelled to the middle of the rows to take the tonic. These white
roots, he called moors.

As Durgin arrived with a load of wicker pot hampers each marked
'James Curnow, Nottingham', Tom Bowman and Harry Carter
told the men how they wanted the sprouts picked.

'Just a handful off each stem,' Tom said.

'And don't rip too many leaves off,' Harry added.

Harry and Tom picked in line with the men on that September
morning. The leaves were wet with the early dew. The pickers wore
gaiters over their breeches then tied a small potato sack around their
thighs to keep themselves dry. Tom Bowman, with sleeves rolled up
to elbow length sported a dark grey woollen waistcoat, while Harry,
who always said he was hot, was stripped to his shirt.

The hampers as they were filled were carried to the headland and
weighed, forty pounds for the sprouts plus eight pounds for the
container. Here Durgin packed the green hard buttons with a packing of newspaper, then some straw which he deftly tied crosswise the
hamper with binder twine. When thirty pots were filled Tom Bowman wrote out a consignment note for Durgin to take to Ayshon
station with the loaded dray and gave him an envelope tucked in and
stamped with a half penny stamp. Inside the envelope was an invoice

for Jim Curnow of Nottingham. Printed on top it read, 'Bowman and Carter, Farmers and market gardeners, Stanley Farm, Ayshon. Telegrams, Ayshon Midland Railway. Underneath the legend, 'Sir, we have sent you this day as follows:' Here Tom had written in 'thirty pots of sprouts'.

Durgin left with his loaded dray. The remaining sprouts were to be stacked under the Cotswold stone wall ready for collection in the morning for Evesham Central Market. On the headland near the Captain's Hill, Harry straightened his back and said, 'Tom, you know we have gone to a lot of trouble getting this strain of sprouts.' At Donnybrook they had netted the stems left for seed so that they could not be crossed by the bees or pollinated by the various varieties of the neighbouring gardeners.

'Ah,' Tom replied, 'Albert Robbins' strain we crossed with our original to get a hardier, tighter sprout. I remember well in 1907, when we first worked together, Albert didn't like selling us that quarter pound of seed. Do you think we ought to sell our strain now, Harry?'

Harry paused and replied, 'Well, we've certainly got the name in Evesham Central Market. Ernest Beck the auctioneer is always glad to see our drayload arrive.'

Tom then said to his partner, 'What's on your mind, Harry?'

Harry looked across the Bredon Hill and around him saw nothing but grassland sheep, a field of oat stubble. The train from Broadway to Cheltenham was just entering the tunnel on the new line under the Cotswolds six miles distant. The whole hill was a remote area of limestone stuck here in the Vale between there and the grey outline of Malvern. Harry spoke quietly for him as if he wanted no one to hear, 'We could grow our seed up here away from the sprouts in the Vale which so often are blowers or open greens, away from the sprouting broccoli of the cottage gardens. No bees will cross-pollinate our strain up here.'

Tom said, 'I'll see Fred Bushell tonight and persuade him to let us leave a patch up here for seed. We need only leave a cluster of sprouts on top of the stems I suppose to grow the blossom and the seed next year.'

Harry then said, 'Let's leave an acre under the far wall that won't hinder Fred with his following crop of oats very much, and I'll rogue them when the time comes.' By rogueing, Harry meant he'd pull up the second rate stems and leave the best plants to run to seed.

Tom agreed, saying, 'It will be a job on wet days for Alf and Jack and Durgin to thresh the seed with sticks on the ballroom floor.'

The ballroom was the granary above the nag stables at Lower farm; the farm where Harry was to live. Called the ballroom because in times past before the reading room was opened for social occasions, dances were held on those pre-1914 war Saturday nights. It was here that Bert Chandler stabled the horses belonging to the dancers in the nag stables below. Mildred had slid her patent leather shoes often on that smooth floor to the tunes of the dance band from Winchcombe.

'Ay, she could fox trot and quick step along of the next,' Bert often said, 'and what went on afterwards was her affair, but Ruby and Percy were not slow in accommodating her, and many a night I had to wait until the small hours afore Ruby saddled his hoss to take her to Cheltenham.'

Michaelmas is a time of plenty on the land, plenty of meat, fruit and vegetables. Apples are so plentiful then the old rhyme goes:

> At Michaelmas or a little before,
> Half the apple's thrown away with the core.
> At Christmas time or a little bit after,
> If it's as sour as a crab,
> It's Thank you, Master.

Michaelmas, September 29th, is also a quarter day and a rent day for farmers. George Gascoigne, the Elizabethan poet wrote:

> And when the tenauntes come to paie their quarters rent
> They bring some fowle at Midsummer,
> A dish of fish at Lent,
> At Christmasse a capon, at
> Michaelmas a goose,
> And somewhat else at New Yere's tide
> For feare their lease flie loose.

The stubble goose at Michaelmas is at its best. It's said that Queen Elizabeth was eating goose when she heard tidings of the destruction of the Spanish Armada. Fred Bushell's geese were almost a legend in old Ayshon. After harvest he let the flock from their pen at the Manor after breakfast. With the old gander foremost, like a team of horses, they walked in line from the rickyard to the stubbles. Hard luck on any dog who chose to meet that party of geese. The hissing of the gander put the fear into almost anything they met on their way.

Fred Bushell and Ruby who farmed the Manor did not provide a rent day like the landlords of the feudal villages. For over at Dumbleton where the Squire rented the holdings to various tenant farmers, the rent day dinner was a grand affair. The landlord, his wife and the kitchen staff provided a great meal for his tenants. They came with cheque book or sovereigns and paid their quarter's rent, complained about broken gates, stopped up drains and bad roads, but received a meal with their neighbours, a real social gathering they looked forward to.

Michaelmas 1911 in Ayshon was a milestone for the village. Two important changes took place in that sleepy nook under Bredon. Harry Carter, in partnership with Tom Bowman, took Lower Farm at a rent of two hundred and fifty pounds a year from Fred Bushell. Harry's house in Donnybrook, that house he built so recently with stables and packing sheds, he left and rented to an Evesham merchant. The move to Ayshon took place on 29th September.

The other change in the village was Jim Cambridge, the Birmingham iron master's purchase of Holloway Farm. Jim had been coming to the village for years to his little cottage in Paris Gardens where he spent weekends from the city. Being a churchman, a keen organist and a friend of the curate, he soon identified himself with the Church and the Cricket Club (the official club). His son, Charlie, an agricultural student, played in the team.

The United Club under Fred Bushell and Arthur Jackson had played a couple of away matches by Michaelmas. They had won one and drawn one. Arthur Jackson's bowling became a legend in the Bredon Hill area. He played for Tewkesbury town some Saturdays and had a trial for Gloucestershire County.

Arguments over cricket at the White Hart were a regular Saturday night feature. Bert Chandler maintained that Arthur was the fastest bowler in North Gloucestershire or anywhere around Bredon. Ruby Bushell who had played for Overbury argued that Walter Green, known affectionately as Bumper, could bowl much faster than Arthur. That hot summer, when the ground was so hard, a fellow from Cropthorne died at the wicket from one of Arthur Jackson's balls which struck him on the temple.

At nearby Overbury, Walter Green was pitching the ball short of a length, proving almost unplayable to visiting teams. The wicket at Overbury was well maintained, a pitch up to County standards, second only to the Dumbleton field. However, the grass was brown from the drought that year, the only green to show on that billiard table pitch twenty-two yards long was the few closely cropped plantains. One such plant grew at the Star Inn end of the wicket, enabling Walter to pitch the ball so that it fell right on that plantain crown. He could bowl his bumpers and make them kick and intimidate any batsman.

Walter, a fairly regular visitor to the White Hart, found himself in the middle of a discussion over fast bowling after a match between Overbury and the official Ayshon Club. 'I hear you spreadeagled the batsmen at Overbury last Saturday, Walter,' Bert Chandler said to him over the after-match pint.

'Oi, Percy Attwoood our captain took me off after the first over, the wicket was so fiery,' he replied.

He then told the cricketers that in their match against the Cheltenham police, he was pitching the ball on the plantain crown. 'The first batsman was a sergeant,' he said. 'A damn great chap over six foot. The ball kicked up and hit him in the jowl, felled him like as if I'd poll-axed him and he showed the whites of his eyes. My God, I thought he was a stiff un. They carted him off to the pavilion. Then I dropped the next ball to a young constable, again on the plantain. He ducked, but he was a bit late and that reeved some skin off his temples. "Bowl the next balls steady, Walter," Percy said. "A man was killed last week by Arthur Jackson's bowling." I did bowl a few lobs to finish the over and Percy didn't let me bowl again.'

Singer Sallis remarked what a pity it was that the cricketers at Ayshon were split into two teams, but Fred Bushell was intent on having a pitch in the New Piece for the United Club.

Bert Chandler then commented on Jim Cambridge coming to Holloway Farm. 'Monied man, they say he is. I'd like to see him buy the Broadenham off Frank Bishop, then the Club udn't be beholden to such a landlord. The Club do miss Arthur in the team. But I got a home to go to. Good night chaps.'

Harry Carter's move from Donnybrook that Michaelmas was a talking point in Ayshon that week. It's true Jim Cambridge did bring more live and dead stock to the village farm than Harry, but Jim Cambridge was not known to the farming folk like the Donnybrook market gardener.

Jim Cambridge's huge shire horses, straight from their iron and steel drays off the streets of Birmingham and the Black Country, were a sight to behold as they left the horse boxes at Beckford station. They came with the Birmingham carter, six of them that Tom Chandler described as 'sleek as oonts (moles), well rubbed up, full of corn.' The drays from the cobbled streets of the city, Arthur said, would be devilish heavy for the horses on the clay lands. 'They ull cut into the grounds with their narrow wheels, a sight worse than waggons made by Jasper, our wheelwright.'

Harry Carter's move from the Donnybrook house six miles from Ayshon did not have to be completed in a day or even a week, if he wished. No railway transport for his goods and chattels, just the two drays drawn by Min and Tommy, Carter and Bowman's nags, and a waggon drawn by Violet and Sharper and driven by Durgin Green. Harry and Tom loaded the furniture into their drays and Durgin brought the stock from the packing shed and the stable.

Since their marriage at Evesham Salvation Army barracks Harry and Alice Carter had gathered together some good solid oak furniture: a sideboard, admirably suited to the great dining room at Lower Farm, a whatnot for their china, a glass-fronted cabinet for the silver, a great hallstand taking coats, umbrellas and a croquet set, the chesterfield, the leather pouffe, fox and badger skin rugs, two Berkeley chairs, two marble washstands, a heavy mangle and dolly tub, a bacon salting lead, brass bedsteads, a small dressing table and a huge mirrored one from their big bedroom at Donnybrook. The kitchen table, scrubbed whiter than white by Alice's continual working with the hard Windsor soap, was always a bit on the big side for Donnybrook, but fitted well into Lower Farm kitchen.

Everything in Alice's house was either scrubbed white or polished, so that Harry could have seen to shave himself in the mirror surfaces of the furniture. The oak corner cupboard was never used for the usual household needs, but housed Harry's cartridges, his decoy pigeons on the top shelf, while the bottom section stored his guns—twelve bore hammer guns, four ten garden guns, rook rifles, and a couple of muzzle loaders.

Alf Miller helped Durgin with the outside effects: wicker pot hampers stamped with 'H.C.', peck fruit picking baskets, ladders, aspragus bundling boxes, bundles of withy twigs for tying the hundreds of asparagus and the dozens of onions, sacks of pea seed, runner bean seed, a bag of his special sprout seed known by him as Robbins Blue strain, the two-tined clay forks, three-tined sword-backed forks, four-tined asparagus forks, Evesham hoes, jadders (a heavier kind of hoe), a skim plough, a pea drill, onion drills, short-sticked onion hoes, raffia, cob harness and crates of fowls. Harry had kept the light legged White Leghorn hens on his Donnybrook land.

As Durgin and Alf brought their loaded waggon to Ayshon they found ample room for everything. The rutches of ferrets—hobs, gills and fitchers, were planted wholesale at the back of the duck-pen. The fowls were loosed in the barn until they were allowed free range after they were familiar with the surrounding orchards. In the dairy at Lower Farm the men put the butter churn and the settling pans for the cream.

Harry's house cow came from his land to Ayshon a day or so later in Fred Bushell's bull float, drawn by Violet. The wooden pegs in the dairy were useful to hang Harry's rabbit wires and the gin traps.

Within a week all was settled in the Lower Farm house, including a galaxy of small useful aids and the tools of market gardening. I doubt if ever there was a man who enjoyed a day at farm or furniture sales more than Harry. He bought so much. 'It will come in sometime,' he'd say. The used implements of the land or the yard he gathered to the last detail. He had packing needles, bagging needles, asparagus knives, spring balances, a steelyard balance, a big bench.

While Alice, that masterpiece of domesticity, bought soap by the hundredweight, tea by the chest, salt by the great blocks delivered on drays straight from Droitwich. The folk of Ayshon no doubt thought that their lines of washing were white, but they hadn't yet seen Alice Carter's. When Alice drove Dick, their iron grey cob, in the governess cart with her two young daughters over to the foot of Bredon Hill a new chapter began for the Ayshon folk.

At the Manor Farm Bert Chandler was due to retire and, as he said, draw the Lloyd George. Ruby had helped him to trim the docks of the breeding ewes in the sheep pens of Paris. They had culled out the broken mouthed old stock ewes. From Barton Fair at Gloucester Fred Bushell had purchased three rams to serve the flock. With raddle powder and linseed oil Bert Chandler made the age old paste to plaster on the rams' briskets to enable them to mark the ewes as they were served. The early ones to come to the ram would be marked red, the ones three weeks later would be coloured blue.

When Bert Chandler came to his cottage on the Saturday night Fanny noticed something strange about her husband. As he staggered under the lintel she thought that he had had a drop too much to drink. As Fanny said later of her husband, 'Ya know, Bert's bin drinking near enough a gallon a day ever since he was hired out at Evesham Mop to Master Meadows of Murcot. He was weaned on the stuff, 'cos he told me many a time that his poor old mother said as how he was fighting for breath with whooping cough as a nipper, still on the titty bottle, and his father gave him a drop of hot cider in a teaspoon. Never looked back since then, our Bert arnt, not to now however.'

As Bert sat in the old Windsor chair by the fire his dog licked his hand and he looked quite pale; a far away look in his eyes worried poor Fanny. 'Have a cup of tea, the kettle's on.' She poured one from the cosied pot, then saucered it for him as usual.

'No, I won't,' he said. 'I've done with cups of tea in this world.'

'What rubbish,' Fanny answered. 'Let me pull your boots off.'

'You can pull 'em off,' he said, 'but you'll never see me put um on again.' Bert sat trembling and shivering in his chair. Fanny asked if she should fetch the doctor.

''Tis no good,' Bert replied. 'I be home for the last time, it's me 'eart. All flip-flopping about inside, gurgling like a stuck pig. Wore out I be.'

Fanny got him to bed and Bert shouted, 'The Good Shepherd's a calling me, he bin calling all day, can't you hear the whistle blowing!'

Fanny said, 'No, Bert, go to sleep, 'tis nothing.'

Fanny sat on the bed while Bert muttered something about the workhouse. 'Don't thee send me to Ampton Addledum, Fanny, 'cos they pulls the pillow from under yer 'ead there and finishes ya. I want to die here at Ayshon under the Hill.'

'You beunt a gwain to Hampton Headland bwoy, I'll look after thee,' was Fanny's answer.

'The Good Shepherd a got a thousand sheep up there and no dog. He wants me. There goes the whistle again.'

'You're dreaming, Bert.'

'I'm coming, Gaffer. Get round um, Rosie.' With this Rosie his dog came upstairs and licked the old man's face.

'Quiet, Bert, 'tis three o'clock and a full moon outside,' Fanny said, sobbing quietly.

'Ho, ho, ho, ho, the ship be gwain over the wall. Back there, Rosie! Sit girl, there goes the tup and he wants raddling.'

'Oh dear, Bert, I'll have to fetch Master Bushell, but I can't leave ya.'

At six o'clock Ruby Bushell passed the cottage on his way to the fields. 'Master Ruby, Master Ruby, come yer quick,' Fanny called from the bedroom window. ' 'Tis Bert, he's middling, very middling.'

Ruby came to the cottage and when Bert saw him he called, 'Give me my whistle off the nail there.'

'Shall I, Fanny?' Ruby said, more frightened than her.

'Yes,' she replied.

Ruby took the shepherd's whistle and gave it to his shepherd. Bert blew three blasts then leant back on the pillow smiling. 'There comes the answer from above. Through the bridle gate they come. Stay Rosie,' he called and Rosie sat and wagged her tail on the mat. 'One, two, three, four, five, six, steady, I got to count um now,' Bert whispered. 'Seven, that unt one of ours, that's a stranger, give me my crook.'

'I'll fetch Reverend Rushton, Fanny, and Dad.' Ruby left the cottage then returned in the milk float with the parson and his father.

'Read from the Book, Parson,' Bert called from his bed. Reverend Rushton took a Bible from his pocket. Bert pointed to the window. 'Over there, sir, under the geraniums, that's the Book, the black un.'

The parson blew the dust from the pages, then read, ' "I am the Good Shepherd, the shepherd giveth his life for the sheep." '

'You understand, sir, you understand, he's got no dog up in heaven, only a whistle. There it goes again.' Bert took his whistle, blew it hard and muttered, 'I be a coming, I be a coming.' Then his head dropped on the pillow. Bert Chandler was dead.

After the funeral at St. Barbara's when the village paid their respects to Fred Bushell's shepherd, Fanny said to the parson, 'Our Bert never drew the Lloyd George pension and he looked forward to it so much.'

'He's left us with a lot to think about, Fanny, and I couldn't help thinking of the time when I visited him and he put me to rights about the shepherding of my flock and how regularly the sheep in the pen had to be attended to by him.'

'The maggoting you mean, sir? Bert laughed so much about that, but he said it to you in fun. He liked to pull the leg at times.'

The day after Bert's funeral Ruby Bushell went to see Fanny Chandler at the cottage. 'We are in a fix with the sheep, Fanny,' he said. 'With no dog, I took Tustin and Adam up the hill this morning to pen them. Adam took the horse whip again, but it's far from satisfactory. I'll have to raddle the rams every other morning. Adam and Tustin would be better employed elsewhere. Could I borrow Rosie tomorrow?'

'I suppose our Bert would have had it that way for he thought more of the sheep and the dog than me, in a manner of speaking,' she replied.

Ruby called for the dog next morning and Rosie followed him up to the bull pen then turned tail and ran home. Back in the cottage the Old English bitch lay trembling under the table all day. She wouldn't leave Fanny as she lay there on an old coat of Bert's.

Ruby Bushell bought a young dog from Kemerton off Mr. Piphens the butcher. A wall-eyed Border collie, he worked the sheep well on the hill. His brother was a champion, folding the sheep on the Overbury estate.

Every Saturday Harry Carter and Tom Bowman took their guns up to the top of Bredon Hill. Saturday to them was recreation, a respite from the daily round of fruit picking, corn planting, hoeing, working the asparagus beds and all the back-bending, heart-breaking work of the day.

Here on the hill, where the brashing soil never clings to the hob-nailed boot, the step of men is lighter, the air is pure and keen, the view of the Vale, the river and the Cotswold Edge a tonic on those Saturdays. Harry took his ferrets in a bag with a little sweet hay to keep them warm.

Alf Miller carried a log spade called a graft to dig out the rabbits. The sprouts in September had been picked over once. Durgin had taken the first pick to Evesham market at ten shillings a pot.

'I wonder, Tom, if the hares have fed on the parsley yet,' Harry said as they passed the quarry.

'We'll see in a minute, slip the fitcher ferret into this holt, Alf, while Harry and I walk to the headland under the wall,' Tom replied.

Alf took the black and white ferret from the bag, put its collar on, then attached a ferret line, placing his furry creature into a hole on the edge of the rabbit bury. As Harry and Tom moved away they heard Alf say as the line snatched between his finger and the rabbits bumped the earth below, 'My eyes, there's some traffic in this yer earth, and the entrance is littered with rabbit currants, their postcards.'

'Look, Tom, the parsley has been grazed and I warrant Sally is in the sprouts.' Sally is a country name for the hare. They walked a chain apart through the rows of sprouts; Harry's dog, Jim, that lissom Italian greyhound, made music among the rows, chasing the hare to the headland. Harry's gun went to his shoulder; in a flash bang, the hare lay among the parsley.

'Give the dog a chance, Harry, I reckon he would outpace a hare,' Tom said and sure enough Jim caught the next one as he gained ground on it in the quarry. 'You'll have to come to dinner next week Tom and taste Alice's jugged hare. She's a cook if ever there was one. Bring Lily along with you.' Tom agreed. 'You know, Tom,' Harry went on, 'I'll be almost living on these hills from now on. I'll bring Alf up here at night with the long net and we'll lessen the rabbits. I'll guarantee Fred Bushell's rent with rabbit money.'

If any man from the Evesham Vale was more fond of sport with ferret, spade, net and gun than Harry Carter it was Alf Miller. He'd poached the Bredon Hills from Donnybrook since he was a boy, but with a wife and family it meant long hours of work on the land for him now. The Saturday sport with Harry and Tom was food and drink for him.

Harry Carter would never say just how many hares he bagged near Great Hill barn from the parsley decoy. The harriers from Tewkesbury way caught a few on the neighbouring farm, but the game hooks at Alan Harding's fish shop in Evesham were for ever full of Harry's hares.

As September closed the last cricket match of the season was arranged as a home match against Dumbleton. Jim Cambridge had reinforced the official club with a couple of his men from the Birmingham Iron and Steel Works. He made himself responsible for the mowing of the cricket field; his cob, Flash, pulled the machine.

Jim's gardener, George, had created a good wicket in the Broadenham, but this Saturday he was away in Birmingham at his daughter's wedding. A lad named Norman worked at the Forge House where the Cambridges lived. He did some gardening, got in the coal and the wood, cleaned the shoes, and was a general dogsbody.

'Mow the wicket this morning for the match, Norman, with Flash,' Jim instructed the lad.

'Yes sir,' Norman replied. He took the pony down to the field and hooked him between the shafts of the mower. As he sat on the seat and circled the ground on that September morning, he had forgotten to do one important thing. George always fitted the leather shoes over Flash's hooves to prevent his iron clad feet damaging the pitch. Norman mowed away until the field was finished by twelve o'clock.

It was then that young Mr. Cambridge arrived. He was captain of the team that day. Tommy's hooves had carved footmarks up and down the wicket so badly that cricket would be impossible.

'No one told me about the leather shoes,' Norman said.

Jin Cambridge's son rode his bike in a great hurry to Dumbleton and so, late in the day, arranged an away match there.

Oh, Ayshon lost on the Dumbleton wicket and poor young Norman had the blame for spoiling the Ayshon pitch.

So September finished in old Ayshon, that Coronation year of early harvest and the death of one of its favourite sons, Bert Chandler.

10

St. Luke's Little Summer

OCTOBER 18TH, ST. LUKE'S DAY, WAS A SPECIAL DAY IN THE
calendar for our ancestors. The time of year had arrived when the
cattle which they were unable to winter would be killed and the beef
salted. The old maxim ran: 'At St. Luke's Day kill your pigs and
bung up your barrels.' Cider making was also under way. It was a
date when the sowing of winter corn should be completed: 'He who
has not sown by St. Luke's Day tears his hair for sorrow.' Another
old saying went: 'Up to St. Luke's Day put your hands where you
like, after it, keep them in your pockets.' A double meaning, no
doubt, that the time of year had arrived when the farmer must be
careful with his money; or perhaps keeping your hands in your
pocket meant the winter weather was on the way.

St. Luke's Little Summer in mid-October brings with it a gentle-
ness of weather. The sun shines on the colourful fruit as it's picked
from the apple trees. The land which has been warmed by the
summer still holds enough of its heat to bring the autumn-sown corn
through the ground, showing the pale green shoots on St. Luke's
Day. St. Luke's was recognised in the past as the day to turn out the
ram among the ewes:

> At St. Luke's Day
> Let tups have play.

Here's good advice for the farmer with the late grazing fields in the
hills, but Fred Bushell, whose apple orchards in the Vale grew early
grass for ewes and lambs, turned out his tups at Michaelmas. It was
also the beginning of what was known as the riding season. Up until
the nineteenth century the church sexton undertook the office of dog
whipper. With a whip he kept stray dogs from entering the church

during service. St. Luke's Day was known as Whip Dog Day from a very strange custom when school boys whipped all the dogs seen in the village street on that day.

St. Luke's in Ayshon in 1911 was a picture of tidy thatched corn ricks in Fred Bushell's rickyard where the grain was as hard as shot after that tropical harvest. In the orchards of the Manor, of Lower Farm and Stanley Farm the apples had that rich red and gold colour. It's true they were smaller than usual, but attractive with a flavour given only by the sun. The orchards in Charlbury hung with Blenheims and sourings which Tom and Harry had begun to pick.

Fred Bushell's cider apple trees bore a good crop, so that this year the mill and the press, now Ruby's responsibility after Bert Chandler's death, ran with vintage cider, a year when the juice had fire from the sun and the alcohol content would be high. It's true the mill and the press didn't produce the vast quantity of vintage this year, but Fred would ration the strong drink to his men.

It was a bright October morning when Durgin Green and Alf Miller drove Bowman and Carter's two drays with Min and Tom, the nags, up Broadway Hill on their way to the apple orchards of Oxfordshire. Harry Carter had warned Alf about the risk of Min falling down in the shafts on those steep hills. 'She is broken-kneed you know, Alf,' Harry said, 'so keep a tight run on her down the hill and always fit the leather knee pads strapped around her front legs.'

'I'll watch it, Master,' Alf replied.

Harry added, 'Ah, Alice thinks the world of Min. She grazed her on the lawn at Donnybrook and now she's at Ayshon Alice likes to keep her in sight. To be quite straight, Alf, Alice doesn't want Min to go to Charlbury.'

The two men took most of the autumn day to reach Charlbury. Their loads of empty hampers, wicker picking baskets and ladders were for them to use with Jack, Tom and Harry. Bowman and Carter had arranged for their men to eat and sleep in a bothy at Charlbury. This accommodation consisted of two rooms over the gentleman farmer's nag stable. These rooms were only occupied in April and May when the hunter mares were foaling and if a horse needed attention during the night, then the groom there could be on the spot. When Alf and Durgin arrived they found a little range for cooking their food, a couple of oil lamps, an outside tap for water and some bunk beds. Jack Gardener, who still lived at Donnybrook, took the London train as far as Charlbury from the station at Evesham. He arrived before the drays, so was able to have a kettle boiling for the men when they arrived.

For some time now Tom Bowman had been riding the motorbike he bought at a farm sale to Evesham at weekends to see his fiancée. 'Shall we ride the bike over the hills into Oxfordshire, Harry?' Tom asked his partner.

'Get your batteries charged, Tom, and we'll travel on the motorbike. What did you say the name was, Bradbury? Ah, we'll ride the Bradbury. By the way, Tom, I told Jack to bring the two Joiner brothers up from the Leys. They worked for me on my Donnybrook ground.'

Tom just smiled at Harry, hoping that he had done the right thing. They already had one Donnybrook poacher in Alf.

Jack Gardener and Durgin sat that evening in the bothy playing dominoes by the range by the light of the oil lamps. 'Where's Alf?' Jack asked Durgin after he had been away half an hour.

'Moochin', up to no good along of them tykes from the Leys. Up to no good as sure as God made little apples.'

'Little apples,' Jack laughingly said, 'they be big, them Blenheims.'

'Thee knowst what I myuns, and it's no good asking the men from the Leys. The only time they deceives is when they speaks the truth.'

Alf Miller and the Joiners walked in bright moonlight through the Blenheim orchards to a spinney over the stream from where, at the edge of night, they had heard the cock pheasants call. Rabbits scuttled in the autumn grass, while on top of a Blenheim apple tree two cock pheasants looked down under the moon. Tomorrow night, Alf thought, when the parish lantern goes behind the clouds, I'll have one of you chaps in my little bag.

Harry Carter and Tom had parked the bike in the yard and gone to spend the night in widow Pitt's cottage. Despite her nursing, her husband Charles had slipped away the previous April. ' 'Twas his chest,' she told the men. 'I gave him onion gruel regular. Bread and rosemary lard with brown sugar, but Charles had never been the same since he came back from the Boer War.'

Before they went to bed Mrs. Pitts asked the young men what time they wanted breakfast. Harry Carter who never stayed in bed after four o'clock was loath to tell her. He looked at Tom.

'Harry will cook that, Mrs. Pitts. If that's all right,' Tom suggested.

Harry Carter had brought with him a part of a flitch of home cured bacon, a box of eggs, tea and sugar and a couple of cottage loaves. At four Harry lit the fire in the oven grate, hung the tin kettle from a pot hook over the burning wood and made the tea. 'Tom,' he whispered, opening the bedroom door. 'Breakfast will be ready as soon as you are dressed.'

Tom descended the narrow stairs to the smell of Harry's cooking. The thick rashers of home cured bacon sizzled in the pan slung from the pot hooks, four eggs fried in the fat, two rounds of fried bread were just being forked into the pan. Breakfast, a good staddle or foundation for a day with the ladders.

Harry slipped out in the dark of early morning and called Min to him in the paddock. Min and Tommy came together to the gate and Min nudged her nose against Harry's jacket. He and Tom then unloaded the ladders, the hampers, the baskets, the spring balances and tripod off the drays. From the bothy they heard Jack Gardener cooking breakfast for the other men.

It was light enough at six to begin picking. The Blenheims hung like Chinese lanterns from the tall trees as the sun rose. Harry and Tom instructed their men how to fix the long ladders in the fork of the trees and how to start picking at the bottom of the tree and work towards the top. Each set, as it was called, was the distance a man could reach the apples to the right and left of his ladder. Then the ladder was moved to another set.

As soon as Durgin had weighed and packed forty hampers of fifty-six pounds each, Alf loaded his dray with Min in the shafts ready to go to the station and load a truck there for Nottingham. As Alf stood with the reins in his hands on the back of the dray shafts, Harry called out, 'Take her steady mind. I don't want Min with broken knees again.'

Tom Bowman handed a consignment note to Alf saying, 'You heard what Mr. Carter said, so don't let Min fall down on her knees on the railway bridge or her ull skin you alive.'

Alf took the half smoked Woodbine from between his lips, grinning and muttering, 'Leave it to me Master Bowman.'

Every day for that first week among the apples in Oxfordshire Alf took the loaded dray to the station at Charlbury. Tom and Harry had returned to widow Pitts' cottage from Chipping Norton on the carbide-lit Bradbury motorbike after an evening with the Salvation Army band. ' 'Tis rabbit pie for supper tonight,' she said. 'Your man, Alf, bought me a couple of rabbits.'

Tom looked across the table to Harry. 'We shall have trouble up here on the estate with Alf's poaching and he's your man. You must speak to him.'

Harry who had used the long net on Bredon Hill with Alf when they were both in their teens, promised to have a word with the drayman.

On the Saturday the men, that is Alf, Jack, Durgin and the Joiners, all went by train to Evesham Station. Tom and Harry travelled home on the motorbike. At the Donnybrook end of Evesham Fred Evans kept a poulterer's shop. It was well known that his shop was frequented by poachers of game. Fred asked no questions.

Alf took a bag of rabbits he'd concealed from the orchard of Charlbury. The few shillings Fred paid him were welcome to a married man on fourteen shillings a week.

'Now my bwoy,' Fred said to the fruit picker, 'when you load the apples at Charlbury Station just consign a hamper to me on the passenger train. A feow apples on top and the rabbits and pheasants underneath packed well down with straw. Yurs a label bwoy, I'll see you right.'

Alf's eyes widened as he thought, 'That ull be better then me bringing the game in a bag.'

Back at Ayshon when Alf fetched his money from Tom at Stanley Farm, he was asked if Harry Carter had spoken to him on the subject of poaching. 'Not to worry, Master Bowman,' he replied. 'It ull take a good chap to catch me as was trained under Tom Payne, the Bredon poacher.'

In a couple of weeks the apples were picked at Charlbury. Durgin and Alf brought their loaded drays to Lower Farm where the hampers of apples were shut down on clean straw in the Old Cross barn under the thatch to keep for Christmas. Harry watched the important operation of tipping the fruit on to the straw. Apples bruise so easily and Harry was intent on sending the hampers of Blenheims into the Smithfield Market at Evesham a few days before Christmas. In a year of scarcity Tom and Harry would be proud to show such fruit alongside the Brambley Seedlings and Pippins from the Lower Farm orchards.

'Fancy a day's shooting, Harry?' Fred Bushell asked as Harry walked past the Manor with his gun, swinging a couple of rabbits from his right hand.

'Any time, Mr. Bushell. You know I like nothing better,' Harry replied.

'Bring Tom with you on Saturday at nine o'clock. We're having the first drive of pheasants in the Ayshon wood.'

Now Fred Bushell's shoot was a modest affair, so different from the big drives of game from the Dumbleton Woods or Elmley Park. Arthur Jackson showed a good lot of birds on that October Saturday to be driven by the beaters towards the rhododendron–lined rides in Ayshon wood. The guns were the local farmers and gentry, Fred Bushell, his son Ruby, Reverend Rushton, Jim Cambridge, Arthur Jackson, Harry Carter, Tom Bowman, Singer Sallis, Harry Addis (Fred's solicitor) and a friend of Jim Cambridge from Birmingham, George Salter. The beaters were Tustin, Adam, Jones and Alf Miller, with four school boys from the village.

The October morning dawned on the almost leafless wood overlooked by Arthur Jackson's Jacobean house and barn. Fred met his friends and neighbours at the Manor. He explained to Jim Cambridge that this was a one man show, an effort of Arthur Jackson's to rear a few birds to provide them with sport in the wood.

'It's not like the Dumbleton shoot, no fancy cartridge belts, no flunkeys to load a second gun. You just stand out there on your own and do your best by the driven birds. Tustin, you are in charge of the beaters. Don't drive the birds too fast, all of a rush in front of the guns. Take it steady.'

Tustin took his beaters to Cank's Bank that elderberry coppice, an outlier from the wood. Every man and boy carried a stout ash plant.

'Keep your stick moving,' Tustin called. 'Mark over!' he called again to the men with the guns in the ride.

A single shot from Arthur's gun downed the first pheasant. Tustin called again, 'Mark over, birds on the wing!'

The flurry of feathers left the leaf-strewn woods as the outlying birds made towards the ride where Arthur put their corn. Bang, bang, bang, bang, and the Ayshon guns hit some and missed some.

Fred Bushell had arranged the guns so that Arthur Jackson was in a central position. He was the best shot. Harry and Tom stood in line twenty yards either side of Arthur. George Salter, Mr. Cambridge's friend from Birmingham, used the best firing piece among the shooters. His Purdy twelve bore, a Rolls Royce in the gun world, was the envy of Tom and Harry whose everyday hammer pieces, products of Steelhouse Lane, were basic weapons, true, but in good hands were accurate guns.

I suppose Tom, Harry and Arthur were more used to the sport with rabbits on Bredon than anyone. As the beaters drew near and the birds rose high above the guns, George Salter was getting restless as he on the flank had had little chance of a shot. A cock bird flying low fled in a curved flight towards Singer Sallis. Before Singer could shoulder his gun, George Salter swung across the line and shot the bird in front of Singer and Harry.

As the beaters moved to the Sally Coppice below Arthur's house, Fred had a chance to talk to his friends. Arthur picked up the pheasants as twenty-four were bagged at the first drive. 'Mr. Salter,' Fred said quietly to the Birmingham man, 'don't swing across the line of shooters with your gun. It does spoil our peace of mind and could make cold mutton of some of us.'

'I suppose I was too impatient, Mr. Bushell, I'm sorry.'

At one o'clock the guns and the beaters all went to Arthur Jackson's house where, in the big long room, Mrs. Jackson had laid lunch. The house, much older than the wood itself, stood on rising ground overlooking the Evesham Vale. The great oak studded front door led into a panelled hall. The stone mullioned windows were reinforced with iron bars. By the side of the front door a pump stood over a one hundred foot deep well. To see those fourteen inch wide floor boards of polished elm in the big room gave an idea of the quality of the building.

Arthur carved the ham and the beef. Mrs. Jackson served the

potatoes and vegetables. 'Nice bit of beef, Mr. Bushell,' Harry Carter remarked as he forked a piece plastered with mustard under his moustache.

'Yes Harry, a little heifer of mine I sold to the Dumbleton butcher and had a hind quarter back off him.'

Arthur told the other guns that the sport would be better after dinner because the birds had been driven into a cover on the Elmley side and if the beaters drove them steady back across the ride they should get a reasonable bag. As Tustin's team made their sticks rattle against the trees and called at the birds squatting in the undergrowth, they rose and fled towards the larch plantation like a skein of geese, but much faster. Ruby, Tom, Harry, Singer and Fred in the middle of the line with Arthur brought the birds down two or three at a time among the rhododendrons.

George Salter, Reverend Rushton, Jim Cambridge and Harry Addis had their share of sport when a group of birds went overhead. Singer Sallis stepped back when George Salter's gun shattered the dead ash keys off a tree just in front.

As the evening light failed and the birds were bagged there was a little spinney to draw above Staights Furlong. From the bracken an antlered buck deer charged towards George Salter. George let drive and missed as the deer passed between him and the vicar.

'What's on, then?' Tustin shouted as he saw the blood stream from Adam's ear and felt a sting in the lobe of his ear. A shot from George Salter's gun had driven a hole straight through Adam's ear, another had lodged in Tustin's. Jim Cambridge grumbled at his friend, Salter, for shooting at the deer and hitting the beaters.

'I'll faint if I see blood,' George Salter said as the men with handkerchieves mopped up the wounded beaters.

'Where do the deer come from? Elmley Park?' Jim asked Fred.

Fred nodded. Jim replied, 'I've written to the General to ask him to fetch them back off my land.'

Arthur, overhearing the conversation said, 'I'll bet he had a laugh about that. Have you considered how to drive a herd of deer? It ud take more than a regiment of soldiers.'

Down in Ayshon village Ruby Bushell took the cowman and young waggoner to the three storey house of Doctor Overthrow, a late Georgian building with a quality all of its own, standing between the thatch and the Cotswold tiles in local brick covered with Virginia creeper, now bright red in autumn.

'What's been going on up in the wood then, Ruby?'

While Ruby explained, the doctor was washing his hands at the brown crock sink in his surgery. He then placed a wooden box of instruments on the table, scissors, foreceps, knives with bone handles, probes and needles. 'Sit back on that chair, Tustin,' the doctor ordered.

Tustin leant back under the oil lamp and Doctor Overthrow took a strong magnifying glass from the box and peered into his ear. 'The shot's lodged in the lobe, Ruby.' Tustin winced, holding his face. 'Now lead is poisonous and can go septic. I must get the pellet out.' The doctor took a probe from the box, he dipped it in an antiseptic solution. Holding Tustin's ear, he ferreted away until the lead pellet fell on to the surgery carpet.

Adam stood by, looking pale and said, 'The shot passed right through my ear, Doctor.'

'I'll attend to you presently,' Edward Overthrow said.

He then put some iodine on Tustin's ear, covered it with pink lint, and a bandage round his head. 'Keep that on until tomorrow.'

When Adam had got in the chair the doctor took the lens and looked at the hole in the ear. 'Salter made a better job here,' he said to Ruby. 'Your father marks his cattle with an ear punch. No need to worry with this, young Adam. You're a healthy young fellow. I passed you for the Sick and Dividend Club a while back, didn't I?'

'Yes sir, and I went to the Feast in the White Hart on Trinity Monday.'

Doctor Overthrow threw a few grains of permanganate of potash in an enamel bowl and poured water until the mixture was bright purple. He bathed Adam's ear with lint, wiped it with a towel, took a pinch of the crystals and put them in an envelope with these words, 'Wash your ear in the morning before breakfast and again at night. See me on Monday and you will be as right as ninepence.' Edward Overthrow then opened the front door. Tustin and Adam left for their cottage homes.

'Come into the library, Ruby, and have a drink,' the doctor invited Fred Bushell's son.

In the library on a shelf among his books stood a handsome silver cup. Ruby lifted it from the ebony stand and said, 'This is rather splendid, Doctor.'

The engraved trophy had been presented to the surgeon for shooting when he was a member of the London Rifle Brigade. 'Yes,' the doctor replied, 'I was pretty good on target in those days and when I was surgeon for the London and North Eastern Railway.'

'Were you now,' Ruby said, amazed at his modesty.

'I don't like talking about it, but with my team the mess we cleaned up at some accidents on the line was pretty grim. I like to think we saved a number of lives.'

'But Doctor, why come and practise at a backwater like Ayshon?'

'Two reasons, Ruby. I like the country folk and partridge shooting on Bredon Hill.'

Ruby smiled saying, 'You put the fear into young George from the Cross cottage, I believe, when you took your gun into his room when he was down with the 'flu.'

The doctor replied, 'Well, I do like to visit my patients at night, see them at their worst. I enjoy the rounds with my pony Lavender when all the rogues and vagabonds are in bed. But I visited George after walking my shoot at the Kersoe grounds where I bagged three couples of partridge. Have a drop of whisky?'

Ruby looked a bit apprehensively at the old gentleman.

'I know what you are thinking,' the doctor replied. 'You've been talking to Singer Sallis.' Ruby nodded assent. The doctor laughed. 'I ordered a brandy at the White Hart and Singer, you know, likes to try and see how much water a little brandy will colour. I like it neat. Well, at the surgery I invited Singer to have a drink when he came to collect a bottle of medicine for Mrs. Sallis. It's true in the surgery I keep whisky in a blue bottle marked poison. I was pouring some from the bottle when Singer called out, "I'm not drinking whisky from that bottle." I said, "Oh, it's just my way of keeping it." You see, I can't keep any in here in a whisky bottle, the boys drink it. Come on, Ruby, have a drink."

With this, the doctor opened a locked corner cupboard taking out a fresh bottle and poured two glasses for Ruby and himself. 'How's married life suiting you?'

Ruby was hesitant, then replied, 'Mildred is in the family way. It's due in April.'

The doctor put his hand on Ruby's shoulder and said, 'Congratu-
lations. Do you want me to look after her?'

'Yes, Doctor, but she's going to a nursing home in Cheltenham to
have the baby. I do hope it's a boy 'cause father banks on a grandson.
It's like that in farming.'

'Don't be disappointed now, Ruby. Mrs. White the carter's wife
from Beckford Hall cottage has just had her fourth daughter. She
was so upset. Then she laughed when I told her it appeared that Jack,
her husband, couldn't get one with a spout on.'

'Marriage is a fine thing, Doctor. Old Bert Chandler always
said, "When you be married 'tis there if you want it and if you
don't you can always put your hand on it and thank the Lord for
plenty." '

'You are talking now young man, but there was a man in Ayshon,
I won't say his name, I had to warn him for overdoing his nature
along of a widow woman up on the Hill.'

Ruby drained his glass. 'Now back to the pheasant shoot. I was
sorry you weren't able to come, Doctor, because I know the high
flying birds over the ride would have fallen well to your gun. Better
than men like Salter. He won't be invited again.'

'I'll come to the Christmas shoot, Ruby, and thin the cock birds
out for your Dad on condition Salter or his like are not there. Let that
be a lesson to you that guns are to be used with common sense. I
wonder whether all the shooters broke their guns at the breech when
they climbed the fences around the wood.'

Ruby finished a second glass saying, 'I won a fair bit of money last
Boxing Day at Singer's pigeon shoot in Townsend Close. Some put
their money on the bird, I backed your gun and won a few
sovereigns.'

'Oh, I like the shoots at the White Hart and the sparrow shoots in
the field opposite. That's when you have to be quick on the draw,
shooting sparrows from the traps.'

Ruby left the surgery that Saturday night and was up early on the
Sunday morning with his new purchase, the collie dog he called
Major, among the hawthorn bushes and gorse on Bredon Hill
rounding up Fred Bushell's ewes. Tomorrow, he thought, we will
plant the winter wheat in Cinder Meadow. Tustin and I will drill the
seed with the eleven furrow Knapp drill Father bought at the

Gloucester Show and Adam can follow with Noble and Merriman harrowing behind.

As Ruby viewed the Vale below from the hill he saw a cultivated scene. This has its advantages over a wild countryside in autumn. He saw a field away towards Dumbleton Hill that had been ploughed in September. It had been a mile of brown earth, but now he noticed a change, as the pale green shoots of a neighbour's early sown corn coloured the earth like a delicate sea. Hard by, the undersown clover in his own field painted the palled stubbles, a promise of next year's fodder for the ewes—a rhythm of colour where the dry seed had greened the yeasty ground.

' 'Tis Halloween tonight,' Ruby thought, 'no doubt I'll see the mangold wurzel lanterns lit outside the cottages.' He pondered by the bridle gate after counting the sheep, 'Bert Chandler lies near the tower. I can hear Tustin, Adam, Singer, Arthur and Jones ringing the five bells at St. Barbara's.' A Cotswold ram clipped the wild thyme under the wall. He looked up at Ruby as much as to say, 'Look after us young shepherd, the old shepherd is gone to ground.'

11

All Saints and All Souls

THE HALLOWEEN FIRES LIT BY OUR ANCESTORS FOR THEIR
great fire festival were believed to strengthen the sun as winter
advanced. The ashes of the fire were spread on the ground to bring
fertility. The custom was to run through the fire and smoke and
throw a stone on the fire, then to run away to escape the black
short-tailed sow. A feast of parsnips, nuts and apples followed.

By 1911 at Fred Bushell's Manor all that remained of fire customs
was the making of candle lanterns from mangolds and swedes with
grotesque, lighted faces and placing them on the cottage or garden
walls. The Halloween parties survived where the young folk
engaged in apple bobbing. That was eating apples suspended from
string from the beamed ceiling or eating them from tubs of water
with their hands tied behind their backs.

On November 1st, All Saints' Day, and the Eve of All Souls, soul
cakes were baked for the poor who then prayed to God to bless the
next crop of wheat; a custom which still survived in Shropshire and
Worcestershire when the children went souling and sang:

> Soul, Soul for a Soul cake,
> Pray good mistress for a Soul cake.
> One for Peter, two for Paul,
> Three for them that made us all;
> Paul, Saul for an apple or two,
> If you've got no apples, pears will do.
> Up with your kettle and down with your pan,
> Give me a good big one and I'll be gone.
> Soul, Soul for an apple or two
> An apple or pear, a plum or cherry,
> Is a very good thing to make as merry.

November 1911 at Ayshon Manor, when the young winter wheat stood in pale green rows in foggy mornings, when the whiteness of the blade of lattermath grass in the meadows deceived the dyed in the wool countryman as to whether the fields were white with frost or dew, was a mixture of the tail-end of summer and the winter to come. The yearling cattle were yarded at the first sign of that bronchial cough known as husk. Bert Chandler, now sadly missed, always maintained that the gossamer spider webs on the early morning grass, nature's November pattern, caused the young cattle to cough.

Fred Bushell and Ruby picked out six of the best of the half-bred Hereford heifers to chain up in the stalls and fatten for the Christmas Fair. The well ribbed up animals, feeding on the lattermath supplemented with a mixture of half cotton and half linseed cake, were forward in condition.

The fattening stalls at the Manor were behind a stable half door, where the top section could be left open on muggy days for ventilation from the heat of six heifers on top rations. The wooden manger was under a hay rack where the fodder was forked from the tallet above. Each beast was chained through a manger ring. The 'T' fastening on each chain had a leather washer fixed between the 'T' and the ring, a precaution in case a heifer broke loose, for if she did she would possibly gore her neighbours. The wooden chog acted as weight to balance the chain and as the chain ran fast and loose the beast could stretch or lie down in comfort on the straw littered brick floor.

'Six nice ayfers you have picked, sir,' Tustin said to Fred Bushell as he forked the sweet hay into the rack from the tallet.

Adam Hunt in Bushell's rickyard drove Noble around the turntable of the horse gear, a very ingenious farm machine, where the horse turned a great horizontal cog which engaged with a small cog on a long shaft. The pulley on the staging above the barn drove with a belt the chaff cutter. Here Tustin and Ruby fed the long oat straw into a trough where the revolving knives cut the straw into chaff. Below the stage the pulley drove a root pulper. Ruby and Tustin threw the swedes into the hopper and this machine pulped them for the cattle. On the barn floor the chaff and swedes were mixed with ground oats and beans from Sedgeberrow Mill and left in a heap to sweat overnight, when the chaff would soften and the mixture made a palatable bait for the heifers.

Tustin was proud of the heifers in the stall. He kept them well littered and saw that the spring water off Bredon Hill ran through the orchard and filled the little individual stone troughs under the mangers. Tom Bowman and Harry Carter came into the Manor yard one morning as Fred watched Tustin carry the skips of bait for the heifers.

'What do you think of them?' Fred asked the partners.

'Don't know a lot about beef cattle, but I've done enough milking seven days a week at Honeybourne to satisfy me,' Harry replied.

'How about you, Tom?' Fred said as he put his hand on the rump of a heifer.

'Oh, I helped my brother, Jim, with Squire Baldwyn's milking cows when I was a boy. Jim was cowman and one cow was so quiet he used to give me a bob up on to her back and I rode from Ten Furlongs to the yard.'

'Beef and corn's the thing. Beef cattle put goodness into the pastures while milking cows take it out. Lots of tenancy agreements forbid the tenant to graze milking cows in some of the fattening pastures.'

'Is that so?' Harry replied.

Tom said to Fred Bushell, 'There was a point we wanted to discuss with you. We would like a bunch of stoves to graze Spring Hill where the grass is pretty rank. What do you suggest?'

'Come with me to Bridgnorth to the November Fair and there you'll buy cattle worth the money. For fourteen pounds a piece you'll get heifers which'll make twenty pound in the spring. I'll come with you if you like.'

Harry nodded, 'I'll leave it to you and Tom. I've got my work cut out with the fruit and the green stuff. That sprout money will buy a bunch of cattle.'

At Stanley Farm Durgin loaded the dray most evenings ready to take the produce to the Evesham Market with Min. The sprouts off the hill continued a good trade. The Blenheims from Charlbury which had been stored were now being picked up and hampered on Wednesdays for Durgin to take to market.

Every week Alice Carter sent a box of her hen eggs and a basket of

duck eggs to market on Durgin's dray. Harry Carter had grown half
an acre of parsnips on his Donnybrook land. Alf and Jack dug a few
bags every week for market.

'Just ask the auctioneer how the 'snip trade was yesterday,' Harry
asked Durgin as he left the yard with a loaded dray. 'All right,
Master,' was Durgin's reply.

After the bags and hampers of sprouts and apples were unloaded at
the market and Durgin had tied Min's bridle to the railings, he went
to the market office where a young clerk, green from Prince Henry's
school, was at the desk. 'How was the 'snip trade 'isterdy?' Durgin
enquired.

'There was a distinct upward movement yesterday, and the trend
was definitely firmer.'

Durgin looked at the clerk with disgust, thinking if that's education, I'm glad I was taught in St. Barbara's vestry. 'I asked thee a civil
question and expected a civil answer,' he said severely.

'The merchants are aware of a distinct shortage of roots after the
tropical heat,' the clerk replied.

'What's the problem, Mr. Green?' the auctioneer asked as he came
into the office overhearing the conversation.

'I asked your clerk how the 'snip trade was 'isterdy.'

'Oh, tell Mr. Carter they made four shillings a bag and we can do
with all he's got.'

'Thank you, sir,' Durgin replied. When he got back, Harry Carter
met him in the yard.

'Tom's gone to Bridgnorth with Fred Bushell today, cattle buying. We shall want you to feed the cattle every morning. So I've
bought a rick of hay off Mr. Bushell, one behind the firs, next to the
sprout field. Alf and Jack can handle the sprouts.' Durgin's eyebrows
raised; he just looked at Harry Carter. 'I know what you are thinking; the cattle have not been bought yet, but I've told Tom to buy at
least twenty and Fred Bushell's going to advise him.'

'How am I gwain to haul the hay from Master Bushell's rick to
Spring Hill?' Durgin asked with his usual worried look.

'Take Captain up there with a muck cart and leave the horse cart
and gears on Spring Hill. You'll have no trouble catching Captain, he
will come to you if you take him a bit of corn.'

Tom did buy cattle at Bridgnorth. When Messrs. Nock and

Deughton's hammer hit the rostrum and the auctioneer called, 'Sold. What name please?' Tom Bowman replied, 'Bowman and Carter, Ayshon, near Tewkesbury.'

Mr. Bushell called from the ring of farmers and dealers, 'If they don't pay, I will.'

Tom Bowman remembered Fred's introduction to the Shropshire market, always finding Fred a keen astute business man, but a fair and helpful neighbour and landlord.

The cattle were driven from the station pens next morning by Durgin, Tom and Harry. They took a road up the hill along Churchway through Grafton to the field of wiry grass and clear springs of water known as Spring Hill. Durgin with a hay knife cut the kerves from the rick and with loaded cart foddered the cattle.

Tom Bowman went every day to the hill keeping a sharp eye on the heifers. He realised that the wiry grass had a softer green herbage under the hard bents. Arthur Jackson, who had similar grass keep, which he had improved, advised Tom to sow salt on the pasture, rendering the grazing sweet and palatable for the cattle.

Harry Carter ordered a truck load to be delivered to Ayshon station. This was hauled up the hill past Paris Gardens, through the Leasow and the gully to the hill grazed by the cattle. As Jack, Alf and Durgin sowed the salt from buckets broadcast on the grass, the heifers followed them licking the grass, licking the bed of the dray where the salt from the bags had been spilled.

Alf Miller, quite amused by the salt sowing, knew perhaps more than most that the Bredon Hill mushrooms would grow even more prolifically on Spring Hill as the ground was dressed with the mineral that suited them best. Alf had made money on the side from the mushrooms off the hill this autumn. While the big ketchup fungus, renowned for its size and quality, was the basis for Annie Green's mushroom ketchup, a condiment prized by the folk of the hill villages for adding that little zest to the broad flitches of fat bacon.

'You are learning,' Fred Bushell said to Tom and Harry when he walked from his fields by the firs to the hill where their cattle grazed. 'I'd suggest,' he added, 'that when the weather is open, free from snow and frost, that Durgin goes easy with the hay. In November the heifers should keep condition on the grass alone, now you have dressed it with salt. There will be another shoot on Saturday,' he added, 'so come along. Doctor Overthrow takes Mr. Salter's place in the guns—no more trigger-happy shots this time I hope.'

Harry Carter's face lit up, he stroked his moustache, pushed his trilby hat back a bit farther on his head, showing a lock of greying hair, then replied, 'We'll be there, Mr. Bushell.'

Doctor Overthrow did live up to his reputation the following Saturday, bagging more birds than the other guns and with that deadly left hand barrel killing the long tailed ones that were out of range to his friends.

Tustin Finch ragged Durgin about his new role as stockman on the hill and whether he could feed cattle and attend chapel on Sundays, or would he give the beasts enough hay on a Saturday to last until Monday, like his pig. ' 'Tis an abominable lie about the pig,' Durgin replied. 'I reckon that when you were born the nurse, instead of smacking your ass to make you cry, hit you on the yud and now you've got a tile loose.'

But Tustin had no tile loose, far from it. In the stalls of the fattening cattle at the Manor, Tustin was worried about a roan heifer. 'Come with me, Master, if you've a minute and look at this heifer,' he called across the yard to Fred Bushell.

Fred with Ruby joined the cowman in the stalls. 'What's wrong? They look all right,' Ruby said.

'This roan, I'll warrant is in calf,' Tustin remarked.

'Now, tell me what makes you think that,' Fred said, a bit concerned.

'First I noticed the other heifers have been on bulling, but not the roan. I've looked at her bag and her tits be waxy. Now I'll show ya, she looks well, rubbed up, I'll agree, but that big belly unt swedes and corn, 'tis a calf.' Tustin with clenched fist drove it into the heifer's side, held his head as if listening, then said, 'There, that's the calf's head.' Grasping the roan's tail and holding it aside, Tustin looked saying, 'Her shows behind too, hers springing.'

'Can't make it out, but I do believe you are right, Tustin. But how did she become in calf?'

'Stole the bull, Master, her did, last spring when they grazed anant the neighbouring estate where that Jersey lies with the milkers. The roan heifer did get out one morning and it looks as if the Jersey bull served her.'

'When was that, Tustin?' Fred enquired.

'Oh, before Easter,' Tustin replied.

'Unchain her, Tustin, and walk her round the yard.'

'Right, sir.'

'Open the door, Ruby.'

The heifer walked around the yard and the three men watched her closely. 'Put her in the loose box,' Fred ordered. Ruby opened the door and the heifer was shut in.

Not many days after, Tustin stood on Bushell's back court and said, 'The roan heifer has calved a nice little heifer calf. Looks like a cross Jersey.' Fred went to the loose box with Tustin and saw the newly born calf and her mother.

Back in the kitchen at mid-day dinner, Ruby called on his father who said how lucky they were unchaining the heifer before she calved. She would possibly have strangled herself when calving with a chain around her neck. 'Sit down, Ruby. Now just take a leaf out of Tustin's book when dealing with stock, be observant.'

He then said how strange it was for men who were deemed to be a bit lacking in intelligence that they so often had an uncanny knack of knowing when something was wrong with animals. Men like Tustin, however gallus, supposedly simple, were the salt of the earth. 'I've known vets trained at the Royal Dick College who have not recognised the signs of illness or anything awry with cattle.'

That Friday night Fred Bushell gave Tustin a golden sovereign extra in his wages for being so observant. 'Keep it quiet though, lad, I don't want it known that I tied up an in calf heifer to fatten for Christmas!'

Jim Cambridge, the Black Country iron master, woke one Monday morning to the ring of falling axes in Ayshon wood. Fred Bushell sold a number of mature oaks to Espley's of Evesham. He also sold that row of elms bordering Carrants Brook in the two narrow meadows known as the Needle Lands.

When the first oak tree crashed to the ground on the edge of the wood bordering Jim Cambridge's orchard he called, 'Emily,' to his housemaid, 'where are they felling trees?'

'In the wood, sir, so George says.'

'George,' he called from his breakfast room. His gardener left his leaf sweeping under the chestnut trees in Mr. Cambridge's garden and came to the back door of the Wynch House. 'Take a message to Mr. Bushell. I have to catch the eight fifty train to Birmingham.' The message read,

'Dear Fred,

I've just heard the news that you are felling the big oaks in the Ayshon wood. Please come along to the Wynch tonight after seven thirty. I'll be back from Birmingham on the seven o'clock train. Kind regards, Jim.'

All day long the ring of the tree fellers' axes could be heard from the wood. The great oaks fell as planned, bordering the rides. The chips from the axes lay cream and clean like tea plates around the butts of the oaks, as the straight trunks were shredded of their limbs. The chips and spauls, or the timber unfit for the mill at Evesham, lay a harvest of firing for the Ayshon cottagers. At one shilling a tree charged by the axeman in the White Hart that night, the men of the land bought enough fuel for the winter fires in the cottages.

By moonlight Tustin, Durgin, Alf Miller, Jones and Adam with crosscut saws and hatchets, cut the firewood or cordwood as it was called, into handy sizes ready for Fred Bushell's dray to take to their homes. 'Two warms we be having,' Durgin declared as he stripped off his jacket in the wood when he and Alf Miller pulled and pushed the saw through the oak boughs. 'One warm now and another, all being well, as me and Annie ull be sitting anant the logs in the ingle at Christmas.'

At the Wynch the evening of the first day of the 'fall' in the wood, Fred Bushell arrived and was welcomed into the small parlour which Jim Cambridge used as a library. The table loaded with drinks of every kind in decanters, carafes, syphons, bottles, sparkled with the Stourbridge glasses in the lamp light.

'It's none of my business I know, Fred, but it hurts me to hear the crashing of fine trees being felled which have been a part of the scene here no doubt since the time of the Commonwealth.'

Fred puffed at his pipe, then sipped the fine port from his glass and replied, 'The trees, Jim, are mature. I am just thinning out the oaks to make way for the larch I planted a while back.'

'Larch, Fred, that foreign tree will never match up to English oak.'

' 'Tis a fine fencing wood, Jim,' Fred replied. 'The rails at the top of Church Close fencing off Paris Hill are fenced with sown larch poles, cut and sawn in Squire Baldwyn's time by Jonathan on the stream saw, and some earlier were sawn in the saw pit at Lower Farm by old Nailus who worked for Squire Baldwyn.'

'You may think me a bit of a crank, Fred, but if you had lived in the Black Country where the giant slag heaps from the pits and foundries form hills against the morning sun instead of the greenery of trees, you'd understand.' Jim Cambridge reached for his bookshelf. 'It was you who introduced me to William Barnes, Fred, when I first started coming to Ayshon. You listen to this one:

VELLEN THE TREE

'Aye, the gre't elem tree out in little hwome groun'
Wer a stannen this mornen, an' now's a-cut down.
Aye, the gre't elem tree, so big roun' an' so high,
Where the mowers did goo to their drink, an' did lie
In the sheade ov his head, when the zun at his heighth
Had a-drove em vrom mowen, wi' het an' wi' drith,
Where the hay-meakers put all their picks an' their reakes
An' did squot down to snabble their cheese an' their ceakes
An' did vill vrom their flaggons their cups wi' their eale,
An' did meake theirzelves merry wi' joke an' wi' teale.

Ees, we took up a rwope an' we tied en all round
At the top o'n, wi' woone end a-hangen to ground,
An' we cut, near the ground, his gre't stem a'most drough,
An' we bent the wold head o'n wi' woone tug or two;
An' he sway'd all his limbs, an' he nodded his head,
Till he vell away down like a pillar o' lead:
An' as we did run vrom en, there, clwose at our backs,
Oh! his boughs come to groun' wi' sich whizzes an' cracks;
An' his top wer so lofty that, now' a'-vell down,
The stem o'n do reach a-most over the groun'.

Zoo the gre't elem tree out in little hwome groun'
Wer a-stannen this mornen, an' now's a-cut down.'

'That'a all very well, Jim, but the trees as they mature must be felled or they become useless for timber. What do you propose I do?' Fred replied, rather bemused at having his own poet, as he liked to think of Barnes, quoted against him.

'What other trees do you intend to fell?' was Jim's next question.

'A row of elms alongside the brook in the Needle Lands.'

'Are they mature, Fred? I'd like to see them,' Jim replied.

'You shall tomorrow, I'll run you down to the main road in my trap and you shall see for yourself.'

Next morning the Squire of the Manor and the iron master walked up the long field of the Needle Lands together, leaving the cob and trap in Thurness shed.

'A fine lot of trees and a rookery, what a shame to fell them,' Jim opened with.

Fred pointed out where the wet had penetrated holes in the trunks, where the gale-blown branches had fallen, and explained that soon the whole trunks of some trees would be rotten.

'Those young trees growing out in the field, what's happening to them, surely you won't fell them?' Jim said.

'Oh, the suckers from the big elms will have to be grubbed up and burnt. They prevent the mowing machine from cutting the grass alongside the hedge, you see.'

'Burnt, Fred, oh no, not burnt!'

'What do you suggest then, Jim?' Fred replied.

'Can I buy them from you and plant them in my hedgerows. I can get, George, my gardener to dig them up and move them,' Jim answered.

Fred who was always ready to make a few pounds replied, 'I'll sell them at half a crown apiece.'

'That's a deal. I'll try and replace in Ayshon the trees that are being felled.'

The two men returned to the village, Jim pleased that at least he would replace the elms in years to come, Fred reckoning that two hundred suckers at half a crown each would be twenty-five pounds, a good deal that morning. Arthur Jackson and Singer, with Ruby, made a great deal of Fred's twenty-five pounds sale for elm suckers in the Needle Lands, but Jim was satisfied in replacing to an extent the fallen trees in Ayshon wood. So the gentleman farmer stocked his hedgerows with elms and instructed his men to leave every ash, oak, elm, even elderberry sapling, which grew in the hedges and trim the low branches to produce trees in Ayshon in years to come. He graced his two fields leading into the village with almond, flowering cherry, flowering crab, which gave a show of colour and scent at Easter time. One sees his reasoning. He, perhaps much more than the natives of Ayshon, treasured the trees, the birds and the wild flowers. Banks of daffodils were planted by gardener George on the Bredon slopes. 'He planted better than he ever knew.'

12

Burying Old Tom

AT AYSHON AND THE BREDON HILL VILLAGES, DECEMBER WAS hailed by the folk on the land as a month of festival. Festivals were few in 1911, holidays practically non-existent, when the men worked a six day week and the stockmen and shepherds had their stock to attend to on Sundays.

Beside the Christmas festivities, the other respites from the regular graft of labour were Harvest Suppers and the Sick and Dividend Club Feast in June. Doctor Overthrow, that wise man of medicine and surgery, had two principal prescriptions for his patients—one for after-Club sickness and another to combat the overeating at Christmas. These bottles of jallop were in demand at both seasons.

Since bonfire night the bells of St. Barbara's had been rung every Wednesday night practising for Christmas. Arthur Jackson was head of the ringers, he with Ruby, Adam's father, John Hunt, Tustin, Singer Sallis and young Adam as a learner. Arthur patiently schooled Adam with the rudiments of ringing that smallest bell in the tower, the treble.

Arthur was very particular about the behaviour in the ringing chamber. He was adamant that the ringers should never wear any clothing like neckerchiefs or loose sleeves which would catch in the rope. More than one village worthy had been hung up against the ceiling in the Vale in Arthur's experience.

Reverend Rushton looked in with his lantern one Wednesday night when the frost had welded the churchyard path to stone. 'How's young Adam shaping?' he enquired.

'Pretty well, sir, we'll make a man of him yet. He's taking over his father's bell for ten minutes at a stretch. We'll break him in.'

'Drop of cider, Vicar?' Singer said as the men drank from the crock tots filled from a jar.

'Ah, just a little Singer. I hope you all have a Merry Christmas when the day comes,' Reverend Rushton replied. 'Are you in good voice for Boxing Day and your carol singing?' he added.

'Never been better. We'll make the village arise with our old one, "Arise ye sleepy souls, arise".'

The vicar laughed, left the tower and went to Fred Bushell's Manor for an evening pipe and drink.

Meanwhile Tom Bowman and Harry Carter were loading sprouts daily for Nottingham and Evesham markets. Durgin took his loaded dray at first light to Evesham Central. Tom followed on his Bradbury motorbike and arranged with Ernest Beck, the auctioneer, to bring a second load in after dinner. Tom Bowman rushed back to Ayshon where Harry loaded Tom's dray ready for two o'clock.

'I'm staying overnight at Lily's house in Donnybrook, Harry, when I've taken the sprouts to market. I'll drive back in the morning.'

Harry suggested, 'Why not take in the Christmas pheasants? They're hanging in my dairy. Then Lily and her Dad and Mother will be sure of the birds on the day.'

Harry shouldered a hamper half-full of apples and sprouts with a brace of pheasants and a hare on top. 'I know Will Westwood will relish some game. I've been out many times with Lily's father when he worked alongside me, but he was more of a fisherman.'

'Ah,' Tom replied, 'Many's the night he sat all night long in his boat fishing tench and pike from the Avon by the Golden Gates.'

Tom took the load of sprouts to Evesham and by the time they were on Mr. Beck's auction floor it was almost dark. He drove over the bridge to Donnybrook, stabled his horse in Mr. Westwood's stable, meeting Lily as she arrived home from where she worked as a dressmaker. As they went into the front room, Mrs. Westwood, all thirteen stone of her, emerged from the shop she kept by the side of the house where she sold the fruits and vegetables of Will Westwood's land.

Tom blinked under the gas lamps of Lily's house. Lily put the kettle on the gas stove and Tom marvelled at the speed with which it boiled. He thought of the fire sticks and the black-leaded iron kettle of Ayshon, and wondered whether Lily would mind leaving the town of gas and shops for the quiet of Ayshon when they married. But after all, Harry Carter and Alice had been used to gas and now were back to paraffin, he told himself.

Lily and Tom spent the evening down at the chapel by the river. Lily was singing in the Service of Song. She helped out in the choir when not at the Salvation Army. Early next morning Tom harnessed the nag and the dray was rattling its iron-shod wheels over the cobble stones. 'Off early Tom.' Will Westwood said.

'Yes, Harry will be about by now, and there's work to do for Christmas.'

Back at Ayshon Harry was out with the men. He called Tom to the dairy. On the wooden pegs hung pheasants, partridge and rabbits in some number. 'Tom,' Harry said, 'all the sprout money you bank, don't you?'

'Oh yes, then we draw enough to live on every Friday,' Tom replied.

'Let's have a bit extra at Christmas, start the bike up and we'll take these to Alan Harding and part the money.' Harry loaded the sidecar, as Tom started the motor, wondering what his partner on the pillion had in mind.

Alan Harding bought the rabbits and game. Then Harry said to Tom, 'What about getting a pair of tea drinkers and some buttoned up leggings, Tom? I'm going to Wyles shoe shop. Are you coming? We've worked hard, I'm sure Lily will appreciate it if you have something new for Christmas. When are you going to name the day, Tom?'

'We are getting engaged at Christmas,' Tom admitted. 'There'll be a party, at Donnybrook. Will you and Alice come?'

'Of course, I've already bought a silver tea pot for you. I had an inkling,' his partner replied.

On 21st December, St. Thomas' Day, the shortest day of the year, known as Thomasin Day, the boys and girls at Ayshon rose early. The five bells rang out over the dark village at six o'clock that morning. The children then went Thomasin. Walking the village street they visited the houses of the farmers and gentry, chanting their Thomasin rhyme.

Here we come a Thomasin,
A Thomasin, a Thomasin.
Here we come a Thomasin,
So early in the morning.

With the added greeting of, 'A Merry Christmas', as the breakfast-ing folk came to the door, they received gifts of money: a penny each or a little more.

At nearby Grafton the children did their rounds Mumping on St. Thomas's Day. Mumping Day in Grafton was a great occasion. The women and children walked the mile to Beckford; here again they visited the bigger houses. Mumping was a polite form of begging. At each house they chanted:

Bud well, bear well,
God send, spare well
A bushell of apples to give
On St. Thomas' morning.

Here they were invited in and given money, apples, mince pies, cider for the women and sweets for the children. At the village school, tables were loaded with sheets, blankets, flannel, all good cloth from Mr. Smith's shop. The women spent their Mumping money on the cloth and bedding.

At Christmas 1911 Fred Bushell at Ayshon Manor tried to keep up the traditions of his father and grandfather. He made sure that no one in the village went hungry at that time. The cordwood from the timber felling was stacked in the sheds behind the cottages to burn in their various fire places. Jane Dunn's Charity coal was distributed from Taylor's coal yard at Beckford station to the needy poor. The two hundred pounds left by this lady produced enough interest to satisfy that demand.

Mildred Bushell was busy at the Middle Farm, making jellies, blancmanges, egg custards and beef tea for anyone who was ill at Christmas. This year she was joined by Alice Carter. Her jellies and blancmanges were easily recognisable by the mark of her mould

—a lion, so pretty for the children to see, was Alice's trade mark in this Christmas benefit.

' 'Tis not the value of the little things we take around, Alice, that matters, it's the fact that the old, the ill, are remembered at this time of the year,' Mildred said.

Fanny Chandler and Alf Miller's wife were enlisted by Fred Bushell to pluck the poultry for Christmas. They sat over the zinc baths in Fred's dairy plucking the birds as Tustin brought them in still warm from the hen house. The breast feathers were kept aside for stuffing cushions and pillows and bed ticks. At the Lower Farm Alice Carter and Annie Green plucked the fowls, the ducks and geese for Durgin to take to Evesham market.

Fred Bushell mulled over in his mind the fact that now Bert Chandler was dead he must get someone to kill the pigs for Christmas. For every year Fred gave his men pork for that day.

'I'll kill them,' Tustin volunteered when Fred mentioned his dilemma. 'I've helped Bert so many times that it will be no trouble for me if I can have young Adam to help me.'

So the morning of the pig killing came. Bert Chandler had always killed the big fat pigs on the farm, twenty score Gloucester Old Spot hogs, burning off the bristles with wheat straw in the yard, when scalding the porkers' carcases. Fred Bushell got the water to the right temperature for the scald in his copper in the back kitchen. Adam held the porkers while Tustin killed them, much as Bert had done in the Christmases before. The two pork pigs were hung from a hook in the kitchen to set ready for jointing the following day.

'There's a sucking pig among the litter with rupture,' Fred said to Tustin. 'Will you kill that one and dress it.'

Young Adam, keen to learn and eager to have a go said, 'Can I butcher that one, sir, 'tis only small?' Tustin handed the knife to the lad and told him exactly where to stick it. Adam killed his first pig when only thirteen years of age at Christmas 1911.

'What you having extra on Christmas Day, Fanny?' Fred asked her as she plucked the fowls in the dairy.

' 'Twill be a quiet time for me now our Bert's gone home,' she answered.

Fred replied, 'I've got a little sucking pig for you. Adam'll bring it round to your cottage tomorrow.'

Fanny's face lit up, then she shed a tear as she sobbed, 'Our Bert, he did love a sucking pig, but never mind, he'd like me to enjoy it I'm sure. My sister's coming over from Bredon.'

And so with ample food and drink, if only for a season, the Ayshon folk celebrated the manger birth. It's easy for the labourers of the land to go along with the Christmas story when the early lambs are born and the stalled oxen warm the air near the manger. The smell of sweetness, as sweet a perfume as anything in nature, is the subtle aroma of June hay.

The hay matured from the rick in the December manger has a quality of mellow tobacco, or the blow of beans in summer; so the countryman's imagination pictured the birth at Bethlehem.

As ever, folk in 1911 were that bit nicer to each other at the festive season. Tustin took Durgin a hare his dog caught on the hill. Durgin knew that the backchat, the leg pulls, the sarcastic remarks of the stockman these last twelve months were the ways of a man undecided about life, the youthful gallusness towards his older associates. So true in Ayshon were these lines:

> Now is the ancient feud forgot,
> The growing grudge is laid aside.

In a time when the music of the village consisted of the church organ, the chapel choir and the songs at the White Hart pub, suddenly the air was filled with music and song. The Tewkesbury Tabber and Tub band played the rounds of the houses. This drum and fife ensemble had been a regular feature under the hill for years. High up on Bredon a German band stayed at La Loo cottage. They played to the villagers of Overbury and at the Yew Tree pub at Conderton.

Through Tom Bowman at Stanley Farm the Evesham Salvation Army Band came to Ayshon playing Christmas carols. They visited at other times in the year as well, forming a ring of bandsmen and villagers at the top of Blacksmith's Lane opposite the doctor's surgery and up near the White Hart. But Christmas was different for they came in the evening and that Christmas 1911 was frosty after the long hot summer.

Tom Bowman played the euphonium while Harry Carter made

music from a great souzaphone. The band was always welcomed by Fred Bushell and Jim Cambridge who was very generous to them.

'Having trouble, Tom?' Fred Bushell called from his front door as a carol was being played on the Manor lawn.

Tom went into Fred's hall and explained, 'My valves are frozen, Mr. Bushell.'

Fred thought it a huge joke as Tom took the valves from his instrument and blew the ice from the tubes. Was there ever sweeter sounds played under the hill? The strains of the well-worn carols floated on the frosty air among the orchards of Ayshon, certain woods and orchards on the hills having an echoing effect. The band of twenty-five strong played all the parts but these were multiplied by the echo from the hill.

A few days before Christmas the overnight snow covered the road from the Manor along Beckford Way to a depth of four inches. Ruby called Tustin to the Manor Barn where one of Fred Bushell's traps stood under the tallet.

'Here, Tustin,' he said, 'give me a hand to take these wheels off the trap.' The two men lifted the one wheel and put a number of railway sleepers under the axle, they undid the hub nut first from one wheel, then from the other, leaving the trap standing on the sleepers.

'What bist a gwain to do, then, our young Gaffer?' Tustin said.

Ruby's eyes twinkled as he answered, 'Make a sledge, boy, to take us to Beckford Hotel.'

Ruby then took two waggon wheel strakes which had been straightened by the blacksmith. Then he drilled some bolt holes under the body of the trap, bolting the strakes to form runners for the sledge. Next he took off the shafts, replacing them with a pole from a mowing machine, so that the sledge could be drawn by two horses harnessed in double harness.

'Which hosses be ya gwain to hook to this contraption?' Tustin asked.

'We'll have the two nags Father bought at Gloucester. They'll move faster than Noble and Merriman.'

When the horses were harnessed to the pole, Ruby fastened two G.O. reins to their bridles and shouted to Tustin, 'Get aboard, boy, and hold the reins.' Ruby sat beside his cowman and soon they were trotting towards Beckford, the home-made sledge gliding over the snow. As they passed Durgin the old man gave them a contemptuous nod as he muttered something to himself about, 'When fools be born, they got to be kept.'

At the Beckford Hotel they stabled the horses, leaving the sledge outside in the road by the tap room door. All day long that December day, Ruby drank whisky and Tustin drank beer. They slept in the bar after a bread and cheese lunch. 'Now for some serious drinking,' Ruby said, as they joined the Beckford men in the evening, playing cards and singing carols.

'Better be gwain home, adunt us, Gaffer?' Tustin said, as Beckford church clock struck ten.

' 've got lights on the sledge, but we'll make a start,' Ruby replied.

When they walked down the steps to the road the snow had melted and turned to rain.

'Can't go home on the bare road,' Tustin remarked.

'We'll ride the horses,' Ruby answered with disappointment. The two men rode home that December night, while the next day they had to journey sheepishly back to Beckford with the trap wheels to collect it.

On the Christmas morning while the bells around the hill mingled from the towers and steeples, Ruby Bushell fed the in-lamb ewes with sainfoin hay. Holy hay he thought as his morning-after mind told him that it was a special birthday and the lambs would be having their birthdays in March and a young Bushell was due to be born in April. He hurried carrying the kerves of fodder to the sheep. He hurried because he and Mildred were having dinner at the Manor. It would be Ruby's job to carve, to pour out the drinks and look after his wife and father.

As he passed the Cuckoo Pen on the way down the hill he saw the footmarks of Adam Hunt on the rimey grass and saw Adam's team at their Christmas breakfast of broad red clover hay. Adam had risen early to fodder his charges in order to join the ringers in the tower.

Adam Hunt was alone on the hill that morning before sunrise. He thought of the past year of Plough Monday and how last Christmas he was still a schoolboy eating buns at the Sunday School party, dancing 'Sir Roger' at the after tea social.

Harry Carter with a white apron to save his Sunday best, was up at four o'clock as usual this Christmas Day. He fed the parlour fire with logs and warmed the Lower Farm house. He walked the orchard hearing a dog fox at his hen roost, gun under arm. He then took a lantern to the nag stables feeding Min and the other dray horses. By seven o'clock, when Alice came down, Harry was asleep in the fireside chair under the ingle.

Durgin fed his team at Stanley Farm where Tom Bowman had left on his Bradbury motorbike the night before to spend Christmas Day at Donnybrook with Lily.

How the Christmas dinners varied from house to house. At the Manor Fred Bushell, Ruby and Mildred had invited Reverend Rushton to dinner where they fed on beef and drank claret.

Harry Carter carved the Christmas cockerel, Alice's Christmas puddings were as usual full of the special flavour. Harry had boiled them in the copper and fished them one by one from the steam with a toasting fork hooked through the pudding string.

At Adam's house his mother fed the little family on the pork from the Manor. Durgin and Annie feasted on one of Harry Carter's cockerels, as did Alf Miller. Annie Green totted out a good measure of bee wine for Durgin and herself at dinner.

The chapel folk held their Christmas service at six o'clock in the evening. The dark-suited starch-shirt-fronted men took their wives with candle lanterns to the little Welsh-type chapel. Here the harmonium rang out the old carols as the young girl organist strained to reach the pedals.

In the pitch pine pew, Durgin and Annie listened once more as a local preacher told the old story of Christ's birth. Previously Durgin had stabled the preacher's horse at Stanley Farm. Durgin was happy that day as he had seen Tustin come from church along with other villagers. He thought this to be an answer to his prayers for Tustin seeing the light. After chapel, a few folk gathered at Durgin's sister's house over the road and sang around her harmonium.

Tustin's work at the Manor had been reduced some days before Christmas. The heifers had gone to the butcher. In fact, the Bushell family were feasting on a piece of beef from the stalls.

On Boxing Night the Ayshon bell ringers all met at the White

Hart, collected a lantern and a bean pole from the pub and began their round of carolling. The voices rang out in the clear frosty air.

Their carols were not to be found in any book of carols. They were the special carols of the hill villages. Here is the 'withy carol', made popular by an old worthy, Aaron Allen, and reputed to have been sung in 1600.

All hail and praise the sacred morn,
Behold the Son of God is born.
Sweet Alleluya let us sing
To Jesus Christ our Heavenly King.

Behold the bounteous gift of Heaven,
This day to all mankind is given.
Oh, happy day, mankind rejoice,
And praise Him with a cheerful voice.

See our Blessed Saviour lay
Within a manger filled with hay.
While spotless innocence Divine,
Did on His sacred Temple shine.

But now the Great Messiah reigns,
Where angels sing in Heavenly strains,
Where Great Jehovah dwells on high,
Above the regions of the sky.

The spirited songsters of the hill had one voice excelling all the rest, the voice of Singer Sallis. The deepness, the richness of Singer's bass was superb. To hear him sing the tune 'Lyneham' to the words of 'While Shepherds watched their flocks by night' was akin to a cathedral organ. He carried the book for the villagers to sign a 'Thank You' for the twelve months ringing, and give a donation towards the ringers themselves.

Despite the hospitality of folk, the ringers managed to complete their rounds that night, their faces rosier than ever from the wine of the fields, hedges and trees.

In the West Midland villages of England, in Herefordshire and

Worcestershire, New Year's Eve used to be celebrated by 'Burying Old Tom', a practice still prevalent in 1856. The labourers had a few extra drinks of the local cider, beer, or home-made wine, and called this Burying Old Tom. The venue was the village inn. There was singing, dancing and general noise and uproar, when a kind of mock funeral was enacted. The landlord had great difficulty in clearing his pub until he treated his customers all round. They then sang their way home, not in the best accents, or voice, or time, but still they sang:

> I wish you a Merry Christmas
> And a Happy New Year.
> A pocket full of money
> And a cellar full of beer,
> And a good fat pig
> To serve you all the year.
> Ladies and gentlemen sat by the fire
> Pity we poor boys out in the mere.

Christmas was over for Ayshon, but the old year was not quite gone. The bell ringers gathered in the tower on December 31st and rang the five bells at ten minutes to twelve. Tustin had climbed among the hangings and half-muffled the tongues of metal with leather mufflers. What a pleasant sound the half-muffled ring made. A sound only to be heard at funerals and as the old year died. Singer Sallis and Arthur Jackson studied and compared their watches. There was a lull in the ringing, as once more Tustin was among the hangings, now removing the leather mufflers. The signal was given, the teams rang in the new year, and as the command came, 'Fire them!' all five bells rang as one bell. It was 1912.

A maiden lady lived in a cottage near the church gates. After the ringers had sung a carol on the village cross she invited them into her cottage to feast on mince pies and wine. Singer Sallis was dark, tall and handsome. He led the way as usual to bring her luck for the next year.

Day
Sparrow